72

THE LOSS OF

The Scharnhorst

THE LOSS OF
The Scharnhorst

A. J. WATTS

LONDON

IAN ALLAN

First published 1970

SBN 7110 0141 3

Published by Ian Allan Ltd, Shepperton, Surrey and printed in the United Kingdom by Morrison and Gibb Ltd, London and Edinburgh

Contents

Preface and Acknowledgements

This book is the first of a new series which will deal with naval battles of the First and Second World Wars. The books have been divided into two sections—(a) Historical, (b) Technical. It was felt that this treatment would assist students in their researches and also the general reader who may not wish to be overwhelmed with a mass of technical data in the narrative. Part 1, the historical section, will explain how the action progressed, giving a detailed account of the movements of each ship. The introduction preceding the account of the action briefly details the events of the war up to the time of the action, explaining how it arose and the state of the opposing forces at the time. Part 2, the technical section, lists the vessels of the opposing forces and their data and any other relevant facts concerning the technical aspect of the action.

I should like to express my thanks to all those who have assisted me in my researches, especially to the photographic staff of the Imperial War Museum (acknowledged as IWM) and the staff of the National Maritime Museum. I would also like to thank the ship-building firms of Alexander Stephen & Sons Ltd, J. S. White, Engineers, Isle of Wight, Cammell Laird & Co. Ltd, Upper Clyde Shipbuilders Ltd (Alexander Stephen & Sons Ltd), Yarrow, Flt Lt Price (for details of the Luftwaffe), J. R. Dominy, A. Mitchell and the members of the Warship Record Club.

PART I
THE BATTLE

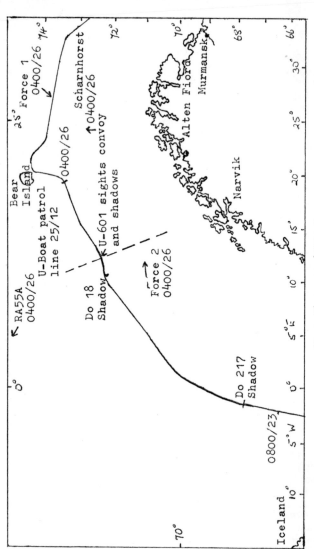

Fig. 2: The passage of JW 55B

Introduction

The outbreak of War

At 11.00 on Sunday, September 3rd, 1939, following the German refusal to call a cease fire and withdraw her troops from Poland, Great Britain under the terms of her Polish guarantee declared war on Germany. The British Expeditionary Force was despatched safely to France under the watchful eye of the Royal Navy and remained on European soil until June 1940 when it was forced, by the more powerful German Army, to retreat across the English Channel.

The first seven months of the war, which later came to be known as the "Phoney War" due to the lack of any real fighting taking place on the Western Front, were certainly not phoney for the Royal Navy. With the sinking of the liner *Athenia*, the battleship *Royal Oak*, the aircraft carrier *Courageous*, and the destruction of the *Admiral Graf Spee* the pattern of the naval war in the Western hemisphere was being set. For many of the men in command the future of the war at sea was all too obvious. Having nearly crippled Great Britain in 1917 with unrestricted submarine warfare, the German navy was later to repeat this process in the war just begun. With a strong fleet of new submarines, and with many more on the stocks and being planned, completely unrestricted submarine warfare was to be carried out against Britain's vital lifeline—her merchant fleet. Not only were British ships to be subject to submarine attack, but also any ship of any nationality carrying cargoes to or from Great Britain. This large submarine fleet was to be supplemented by extremely powerful warships built to act independently as commerce raiders with a large radius of action, a high speed and powerful armament (*viz Bismarck, Admiral Graf Spee, Admiral Hipper* and *Scharnhorst*). These warships were to be backed up by a number of fast merchant ships, specially built just before the war so that they could be adapted to carry guns, torpedoes, mines and aircraft to act as raiders disguised as merchant ships. These raiders and warships were to be supported by a fleet of supply vessels stationed in the ocean wastes.

The convoys sail

In view of the menace to Britain's merchant fleet from the German submarines, plans had already been made before the war to institute the convoy system which had proved so effective in previous centuries. The first convoy had in fact already left Gibraltar on September 2nd, 1939, and was closely followed by another from the Clyde three days later. To discriminate between the convoys, and to show the direction in which each was travelling, they were all given a letter and number, e.g., HX 75 (a convoy from Halifax, Nova Scotia to Great Britain), OG 21 (a convoy from Great Britain to Gibraltar). Due to the lack of escorts and their short endurance, convoys across the Atlantic to Great Britain were escorted by converted merchant vessels armed with outdated guns, e.g. the *Jervis Bay*. Those convoys outward bound from Great Britain were protected by escorts from the Home Fleet to a distance of about 300 miles, where they turned round and escorted an inward bound convoy to a British port. After the escorts had left, the outward bound convoy then dispersed, the merchant ships proceeding independently to their destinations. This proved to be the most dangerous part of the journey as the U-boats waited in the areas where the escorts left the convoy and pounced on the helpless merchant ships, sinking large numbers of them.

Operation Barbarossa

On June 22nd, 1941, the German Wehrmacht marched into Russia. Never before had anything comparable been seen in battle. Whole Russian armies were captured and destroyed. By the end of December 1941, Russian losses were estimated to be 5 to 7 million with 3 to 5 million POW's, 21391 tanks and 32541 guns destroyed. It was inconceivable that any army could sustain such losses and still be capable of fighting back, but the Russians did so. With the aid of the Russian winter, the troops managed to stop the Germans before Moscow and Leningrad. The loss of men and material was tragic but these could have been readily replaced from the vast Russian resources. The subsequent loss of the large industrial centres of Minsk, Kharkov, Kiev, Smolensk, etc., proved to be more disastrous.

To compensate for loss of production and to make good some of the losses sustained by the Russians, the British and American leaders decided to send a fact-finding mission to Moscow to investigate in what manner they could best aid the Russians. The combined British and American fact-finding mission, including Lord Beaverbrook and Mr Averill Harriman, arrived in Moscow on September 28th, 1941. The Russians refused to supply information regarding their losses, but an agreement was reached and signed on October 4th to cover the period October 1941 to June 1942, and thereafter to be renewed annually on that date. It was agreed that Britain and America would, under the first agreement, send 400 aircraft a month (300 fighters, 100 bombers), 500 tanks and 200 Bren-gun carriers a month, 22000 tons of rubber, 41000 tons of aluminium and 3860 machine tools and large quantities of food, medical supplies and raw materials.

The Admiralty had already commenced arrangements to send convoys to Russia by the time the agreement was signed. In fact on September 29th, 1941, on Mr Churchill's personal orders, the Admiralty despatched to Russia the first PQ convoy—PQ 1—carrying 450 aircraft, 22000 tons of rubber, 3 million pairs of boots and large quantities of tin, aluminium, lead, jute and wool.

On October 6th, 1941, the Prime Minister, Mr Churchill, telegraphed to the leader of the Soviet Union (Premier Joseph Stalin) the contents of the October convoys.

viz—

20 heavy tanks
193 fighter aircraft } to arrive at Archangel on October 12th

To sail October 12th and arrive October 19th, 1941

140 heavy tanks
100 Hurricane aircraft
200 Bren-gun carriers
200 anti-tank rifles and ammunition
50 2pdr guns and ammunition

To sail October 22nd, 1941

200 fighter aircraft
120 heavy tanks

(NB these figures do not include supplies sent by America)

It was thus planned to send vast quantities of material to the Soviet Union in outward bound convoys lettered PQ and homeward bound convoys designated QP. Originally it had been planned to send convoys from Britain every 40 days. Early in October, however, Mr Churchill made a request to shorten the cycle to 10 days (see proposed dates of sailing in table above) so that more supplies could be sent to Russia. It was planned to send the convoys to the White Sea port of Archangel where the dockside facilities were the best available. By December, however, it was realised that Archangel would be practically useless during the winter months as the sea was frozen solid and the Russian icebreakers had difficulty in keeping the port open. The convoys had no alternative but to use the port of Murmansk in the Kola Inlet, which was really only a collection of wooden wharfs with a few antiquated cranes to handle their supplies.

The Russian convoys

Up to March 1942 a total of 110 merchant ships had sailed in convoys to Russia and only one merchant ship had been lost. By March 1942 the convoys began to get larger as the Americans started sending increased quantities of supplies. The days lengthened as the months passed and all too soon the perpetual daylight of the Far North arrived. By now the convoys were so large (often over 40 merchant ships) and such vast quantities of supplies were being sent to bolster the quickly reviving Russian Army, that the Germans could not afford to ignore them any longer. The indications showed that the Russians were preparing for a great offensive, as soon as the thaw was over, and as a result the attacks on the Russian convoys began in earnest. Many bitter battles were fought in the sub-zero temperatures of the Arctic wastes, and many fine ships sunk, their crews drowning or dying of exposure. The battleship *Tirpitz* and the heavy cruiser *Admiral Hipper* were sent to the Norwegian port of Trondheim with the pocket battleship *Admiral Scheer*. In March 1942 the *Tirpitz* sailed against convoy PQ 12 but the operation was unsuccessful and the convoy escaped. The next convoy to sail, PQ 13, was not so fortunate. In addition to attacks by U-boats and surface vessels the crews of the merchant ships in PQ 13 had to sustain themselves against round the clock bombing attacks from the airfields in Norway only 200 miles away.

With the threat to the convoys growing daily, and the problems of attack becoming easier with the lengthening days, the Admiralty expressed a wish to cease running the convoys during the summer months. Owing to the desperate plight of the Russian armies suffering further severe losses under a new German offensive, Mr Churchill had to override the Admiralty and convoys of 25 to 35 ships continued to sail to Russia under the ever increasing fury of enemy attacks.

On June 27th, 1942, convoy PQ 17 sailed from Iceland bound for

Archangel and proved to be the most disastrous. After having been ordered to disperse by the Admiralty on July 14th, due to a threat of surface attack by the *Tirpitz*, only 10 of the 33 merchant ships that originally made up the convoy reached Russia. The remaining 23 ships were all sunk by U-boats or aircraft. Convoy PQ 17 was followed by PQ 18 in September 1942 and this convoy too suffered a number of losses.

After such heavy losses, the Arctic convoys were suspended for a short time. This was mainly due to the fact that most of the escorts for the Russian convoys were drawn from the Home Fleet and these vessels were now required for Operation Torch—the Allied landings in North Africa.

Weather conditions in the Arctic

With the winter of 1942 well advanced, and most of the Luftwaffe squadrons in Norway transferred either to the Russian front or to the Mediterranean, it was decided to resume the Arctic convoys. With the threat of air attack much reduced, and the almost perpetual darkness of the winter day, the strong anti-aircraft defence was no longer the necessity for the convoys that it had been, and in some ways conditions were better. The winter certainly afforded a measure of protection against air attack by the Germans, but not against the elements. Severe gales and mountainous seas smashed incessantly against the small ships, the spray from the waves freezing in the air and lashing men's faces like a whip. A freezing sea often coated the ships in ice, dangerously affecting their stability and the operation of equipment, and forcing the crews out on to the decks to chip away at the ice with shovels and axes.

Although the darkness afforded some measure of protection against air attack, it did not prevent the U-boat "Wolf Packs" from gathering around the convoys. In fact a U-boat attack was materially assisted by the darkness. Crews of ships unfortunate enough to be sunk had to rely on rescue immediately. Once in the freezing water they were lucky enough to stay alive for three minutes, and for those in open boats the suffering was unimaginable. The escorts could not stop to pick up the crews of sunken ships as this dangerously weakened the protective screen of the convoy, and so each Arctic convoy was provided with a rescue ship. This was a ship specially fitted out with extra bunks and medical facilities. It was intended that she alone would go back to rescue the crews of sunken ships.

The weather proved to be a more implacable foe than the Germans. During the winter months the ice cap from the North Pole spread slowly southwards, forcing the convoys nearer and nearer to Norway. At times it extended right down to Bear Island, forcing convoys to sail south of the island—to within 250 miles of Altenfiord—where Admiral Raeder stationed his heavy warships ready for a quick foray against an inviting target. The other main problem for the convoys was the distance. From Iceland to Murmansk the convoy route was between 1400 and 2000 miles long, a distance over which there were no friendly bases. As the endurance of the escorts was not enough to take them all this distance every convoy to Russia had to include an oil tanker that could refuel the escorts.

The convoys resume sailing

The first convoy to sail on the new cycle after the completion of Operation Torch was JW 51. It had been decided to renumber the convoys to Russia giving the outward bound ones a JW prefix and the homeward bound convoys an RA prefix. Admiral Tovey, the C-in-C of the Home Fleet, did not agree with the Admiralty view that one large convoy of 35 ships with a large escort—such as PQ 18—was feasible. He believed that a smaller convoy with adequate escorts was far easier to manoeuvre under air attack, and might easily escape detection. A large convoy was also easily dispersed in bad weather, which would cause many problems such as finding stragglers and identifying radar echoes in a melee. Adm Tovey's view was accepted, and so the new cycle of convoys was henceforth run in two sections about a week apart, and numbered A and B respectively.

The first of the new series of convoys to sail was JW 51A, which left Loch Ewe on December 15th. The second half of this convoy—JW 51B—left on December 22nd and its detection led to an important battle. The Germans had decided to attack the next convoy that sailed with the *Admiral Hipper*, *Lutzow* and six destroyers. The operation was a fiasco, the destroyer escort of the convoy frustrating every attempt by the German ships to attack the convoy. The Germans returned to harbour and reported their failure to attack the convoy. Hitler was beside himself with rage over the operation and immediately ordered the scrapping of all the navy's heavy warships. Adm Raeder, C-in-C of the Kriegsmarine, sent a long memorandum to Hitler explaining that the advantages in material and personnel to be gained by scrapping the battle fleet would, in fact, be very light.

Hitler could not be persuaded to change his mind. So Adm Raeder resigned on January 30th, 1943, and was succeeded by Adm Doenitz, who had been C-in-C of the U-boats.

Within a very short time he too was trying to persuade Hitler to rescind his order to scrap the battle fleet, and to some extent he succeeded. In a meeting with Hitler on February 26th, 1943, Adm Doenitz stated that he felt that the convoys to Archangel would make excellent targets for the heavy ships, and that as supplies from these convoys were making their way to the Eastern front he meant to exploit the possibilities of attack on these convoys to the utmost. To this end he asked permission to move the *Scharnhorst* from the Baltic to Norway to join the *Tirpitz*, *Lutzow* and six destroyers. The *Admiral Hipper*, *Leipzig* and *Koln* had, however, already been decommissioned.

Hitler agreed, and so the *Scharnhorst* joined the forces in Norway. All three vessels (*Lutzow*, *Scharnhorst*, *Tirpitz*) were sighted in Altenfiord in March 1943, and with the days lengthening Adm Tovey requested that the Arctic convoys cease for the duration of the summer. The Admiralty also had good reason for wishing to cease sailing the convoys. The battle against the U-boats in the Atlantic was now reaching a climax and many of the escorts in the Home Fleet used for escorting the Arctic convoys were being lent to the Western Approaches Command to escort convoys in the Atlantic. Consequently it was agreed that the Arctic convoys should be suspended during the summer months of 1943.

The winter of 1943
On September 6th, 1943, the *Scharnhorst*, *Tirpitz* and 10 destroyers left their Norwegian base to bombard the island of Spitzbergen. The gunnery of the *Scharnhorst* was so atrocious that on returning to port her Captain (Capt Huffmeier) immediately put to sea again for gunnery exercises. While the *Scharnhorst* was at sea British midget submarines attacked the *Tirpitz* in her anchorage on September 22nd, wrecking her engines and putting her out of action, at least until April 1944 according to the report of the German Naval Staff. On September 23rd, the *Lutzow* left Altenfiord for the Polish port of Gdynia, in the Baltic, to begin an extended refit. This left just the *Scharnhorst*, six destroyers of the 4th Destroyer Flotilla and about 24 submarines.

With the threat from the German squadron in Norway greatly

reduced, and further persistent demands from the Russians to [the] Government to restart the Arctic convoys, the Admiralty agree[d] [to] commence sailing the convoys, but under the system begun i[n] 1942. The new C-in-C of the Home Fleet, Adm Fraser, was o[f the] same opinion as his predecessor, Adm Tovey, that to send 40 merc[hant] ships a month to Russia in one convoy, as promised by the Go[vern]ment, constituted too much of a risk, and so the convoys were aga[in] sailed in two sections.

The new cycle commenced on November 1st, 1943, with the sailing of RA 54A (13 empty merchant ships) from Archangel which consisted of ships that had been left in the port since the previous April. This homeward bound convoy was followed by the sailing of the first section of the outward bound convoy, JW 54A (18 merchant ships), on November 15th. The convoys were to be protected by a through escort of destroyers and escort vessels with a local escort to cover the ships at each end of the sea passage. The convoys would be given a close cover of cruisers while on the most dangerous part of the route south of Bear Island. A strong distant cover would be provided by a battleship force from the Home Fleet under command of the C-in-C Home Fleet. This force would patrol an area from 10° E longitude and about 200 miles SW of Bear Island. It was arranged that the east and westbound convoys should pass each other in the area of Bear Island so that the battleship and cruiser forces could cover both convoys, thereby affording an economy in the use of heavy warships.

Between November and the middle of December 1943 three eastbound convoys (JW 54A, JW 54B, JW 55A) and two westbound (RA 54A, RA 54B) were sailed without the loss of a single merchant ship. The weather conditions were quite good for the time of the year and the Germans ignored the convoys, except for an occasional submarine attack.

Although it was not attacked, convoy JW 55A had been sighted and reported to the German Naval Staff. The fact that the convoy had been sighted decided the C-in-C Adm Fraser to extend the battleship cover right through to Kola, as he felt that an attack by surface forces was quite probable. In his flagship, the *Duke of York*, Adm Fraser went on to Vaenga, where he met the Russian C-in-C of the Northern Fleet, Adm Arseni Golovko, and had talks with him regarding the convoys. Arriving on December 16th, Adm Fraser left two days later and proceeded to Akureyri in Iceland to fuel.

Convoy JW 55A completed its journey without incident, 12 merchant ships arriving at Kola inlet on December 21st, and seven at Archangel on December 22nd.

The day after Adm Fraser left Vaenga, December 19th, Adm Doenitz was in conference with Hitler and informed him that the *Scharnhorst* and the 4th Destroyer Flotilla would attack the next convoy that sailed for Russia, "if a successful operation seems assured". The conference lasted two days, December 19th and 20th, but the most important point to emerge was the decision to attack the next convoy to Russia.

The next convoy to sail for Russia was in fact JW 55B and it left Loch Ewe on December 20th.

CHAPTER ONE

The Convoy sails

On December 4th, 1943, the Admiralty sent the first of a set of signals to gather together the merchant ships for a new convoy. These ships, at that time on their way across the Atlantic to Britain, were to reload on arrival with cargoes destined for Russia. Convoy JW 55B was born.

The ships were ordered to sail from their ports of loading, ports such as Hull, Middlesbrough, Birkenhead and the Clyde, in local convoys so as to arrive at their point of departure in Loch Ewe by not later than the afternoon of December 17th. It was planned to sail the convoy—JW 55B—on December 19th, under the protection of a local escort of the destroyer *Scimitar* from Western Approaches Command, and the *Hound* (SO of local escort) and *Hydra*, two mine-sweepers from the 18th M/S flotilla. The through escort was to consist of the *Gleaner* (SO) a minesweeper, the *Whitehall* and *Wrestler* two destroyers, and the *Honeysuckle* and *Oxlip* two corvettes. It was decided on December 10th to replace the *Scimitar* by the two corvettes *Borage* and *Wallflower*, and on the 16th the destroyer *Scourge* replaced the *Obdurate* in the destroyer escort of the convoy.

Although the convoy was due to sail on December 19th the weather conditions were so atrocious that sailing was postponed until the following day. The senior officers of the escort attended a conference at Loch Ewe on December 20th, at which details for the forthcoming operation were given. The destroyer escort was to consist of the destroyers—*Onslow* (D 17), *Scourge* (replacing the *Obdurate*), *Onslaught*, *Orwell*, *Impulsive*, *Iroquois*, *Haida* and *Huron*. At the conference the officers were told that all merchant ships in the convoy were capable of a speed of 10 knots and that the escorts were to rendezvous with the convoy at approximately 64° N, when the local escort would leave.

The escorts were informed that the cruiser cover, Force 1, would cover the two convoys, JW 55B and RA 55A, in the area of the Barents Sea and that Force 2, providing the heavy battleship cover, would sail from Akureyri in Iceland to cover JW 55B from 027° to 038° E, and then return to Scapa Flow covering RA 55A. The escorts were also told that a British submarine would be on patrol off Altenfiord, to watch and report any movement by the German Battle·Group based there. Following the conference the *Onslow* sailed independently at 17.00 for Skaalefiord in Iceland.

Following the convoy meeting during the morning, at which the captains of the merchant ships were given their instructions about the sailing of the convoy, weather conditions likely to be met, etc., the convoy, under Cdre Rear-Adm M. W. S. Boucher, weighed anchor and sailed from Loch Ewe at 15.00 on December 20th. Owing to a defect in her engines the *Hydra* was unable to sail with the escort but left Loch Ewe later that day, at 23.25, to catch up with the convoy.

As soon as they were clear of the defence booms, the convoy of 18 ships formed into two columns to sail through the narrow passage of the North Minch, at a reduced speed of $8\frac{1}{2}$ knots.

On board the *Belfast*, the flagship of the 10th Cruiser Squadron, anchored in the Kola Inlet, a meeting of the commanding officers of Force 1 and the escorts of RA 55A and the ships masters scheduled for 17.00 commenced at 19.00. The meeting, attended by SBNO North Russia, ended an hour later at 20.00 and the officers dispersed to their respective ships to begin preparations for sailing.

December 21st, 1943

At 08.00 on December 21st, JW 55B formed into a normal cruising position of six columns in line abreast (see fig. 13), having passed through the Minches overnight. Having successfully negotiated this dangerous passage, the speed of the convoy was increased by one knot, to $9\frac{1}{2}$ knots. During the morning the ships were put through their convoy drill, both escorts and merchant ships testing their close range A/A weapons in case of air attack, and the convoy doing emergency turns used in cases of attack by enemy forces during the daytime. As most of the merchant ships had already sailed in convoys either across the Atlantic or to Russia, these exercises were no novelty to the crews, who performed them exceedingly well.

The destroyer escort for JW 55B arrived at Skaalefiord at 09.00 to be followed by the *Onslow* at 10.15. At 10.45 the local escort of JW 55B was informed by the C-in-C Rosyth that a Beaufighter would attempt to locate the convoy in the afternoon, and the SO of the escort was to signal the estimated position of JW 55B. By noon the wind was blowing from the SSE at force 4, with visibility 6, the sky generally cloudy and the sea running at 24. During the day JW 55B sighted both a RN Tarpon and Catalina aircraft and at 15.00 the RAF Beaufighter, that had been attempting to locate the convoy.

The *Hound* signalled the position of the convoy to the Beaufighter, and also an estimated position of the convoy for 08.00 on December 22nd. At 16.00 the convoy was again drilled in manoeuvres; this time it was emergency turns to be taken in case of U-boat attack during the hours of darkness. During the afternoon of December 21st the CO's of the destroyer escort attended a conference on board the *Onslow* in Skaalefiord, sailing at 23.45 to rendezvous with the convoy. Earlier in the evening, at 21.57, the local escort of JW 55B had been told to expect a Sunderland flying boat from No. 18 Communications Group the following day. The flying boat was to provide them with A/S escort during daylight hours.

The convoy detected, December 22nd, 1943

During the night of December 21st/22nd, the *Ocean Valour* and *John Abel* in the port wing column omitted to carry out an alteration of course from 002° to 017°. They proceeded on a course of 002° and became detached from the convoy. The *Whitehall* was sent to locate the missing ships, and the speed of JW 55B was reduced to 8 knots until they rejoined.

At 09.20 the *Hydra* caught up with the convoy and at 10.30 on the 22nd the *Whitehall* was detached from the escort to refuel from the tanker *British Statesman*. The Sunderland flying boat carrying out A/S patrols for the convoy was signalled from the *Hound* at 10.30 and given the position of the convoy. Half an hour later, at 10.59, the *Gleaner* at position R on the escort screen sighted an aircraft passing astern of the convoy, which was still on its course of 017°. The *Gleaner* estimated that the course of the aircraft was 090°, and that it was probably a German Do 217. The aircraft, on a meteorological flight, reported a force of 40 troop transports with an escort of cruisers and, presumably, an aircraft carrier, off the Faeroe Islands. The report was received by Flag Officer Group North, Adm Schneiwind, who thought that a raid on Norway was imminent, and ordered the seven submarines of Group Eisenbart, then on patrol off Bear Island, to concentrate off Vest Fiord. The responsibility for shadowing the convoy, and reporting any enemy forces within 300 miles of it, was given to the Luftwaffe, while the Battle Group was brought to three hours' notice for steam. Some time later, however, it was decided that the ships reported were not destined for a raid on Norway, but were part of a normal convoy bound for North Russia. Group Eisenbart was then ordered to redispose itself on patrol in Bear Island Straight, instead of off Vest Fiord.

By mid-day the weather had begun to deteriorate, the wind still from the SSE had increased to between force 4 and 5, and the visibility remained at 6 with a generally cloudy sky. The sea, however, had increased to 43. At 12.25 the escorting Sunderland closed the Fleet destroyers heading for the convoy rendezvous, and reported the convoy bearing 352° at a distance of 24 miles. Captain McCoy then altered course to 000° spacing the destroyers 2 miles apart to aid in intercepting the convoy, at the same time increasing speed to 18 knots. By 12.30 the *Whitehall* had finished refuelling from the *British Statesman*, but the heavy swell that had risen was causing the oil tanker to yaw so badly that the *Wrestler* was unable to refuel from her. At 13.15 the Sunderland returned to the convoy and passed the position of the 17th Destroyer Flotilla to the *Hound*.

The *Onslaught* sighted JW 55B on a bearing of 027° at 14.00, and the escorts formed up around the convoy at 15.00, Capt McCoy taking over the senior escort from the *Hound*, which was detached from the convoy at 15.15. The *Hound* and the local escort then proceeded independently to Skaalefiord in Iceland. Before departing at 17.00 the Sunderland was given the position of the convoy and a bearing of 016° and a speed of 10 knots, a speed which had been maintained for most of the past 24 hours, and which was one knot faster than the speed estimated by the C-in-C Rosyth, to whom the Sunderland passed the information just received.

At 20.47 when in the approximate position 64° 41′ N–4° 08′ W the *Hound* heard an aircraft circling overhead in the darkness, but it was unidentified and flew off on a course of 340°.

December 23rd, 1943

The situation on December 23rd was still fairly static, the destroyer *Wrestler* being sent to refuel at first light, casting off from the tanker at 13.30. Convoy JW 55B was still being shadowed, while RA 55A which had sailed from the Kola Inlet at 10.45 on December 22nd remained undetected. The C-in-C Home Fleet in the *Duke of York*, with Force 2 in company, arrived at Akureyri on the North coast of

Iceland during the day to refuel. At 01.00 Force 1, which was providing the Close Cruiser cover to JW 55B and RA 55A, left Kola Inlet and sailed for its patrol area east of Bear Island. During the morning the wind increased to force 7 from the SW and towards evening began veering round to the NE.

The A/S escort scheduled for the 23rd was a Catalina of Communications 18 Group Recce which would cover the convoy from 09.15 until darkness fell. In position L at 11.40, the *Orwell* sighted two Do 217 aircraft heading for the port bow of the convoy. They closed, flying down the port side and took up a shadowing position astern of the convoy. At 11.45 Capt McCoy sent a signal to the SBNO North Russia, informing him that JW 55B was still being shadowed, and that the *Haida* and *Iroquois* had opened fire and hit and damaged the aircraft that were shadowing the convoy. The damage to the aircraft was not severe, however, as they continued to shadow the convoy, taking cover in the clouds whenever fire was opened on them. The Catalina detailed to give the convoy A/S protection finally arrived at 13.30, and took up position ahead of the convoy for the remaining three hours of its patrol.

The plan of action

Admiral Fraser called a conference of the CO's of the ships of Force 2 on December 23rd and outlined his intentions and assumptions for the forthcoming patrol. It was his conviction that having escorted convoy JW 55A safely to Russia, the *Scharnhorst* would be bound to sortie and attempt an attack on convoy JW 55B. Force 2 had by this time been together almost a fortnight and the C-in-C had lost no opportunity in giving his squadron exercises in night encounters with an enemy. The officers and men in the ships knew each other well by now but Adm Fraser still felt it necessary to stress that everyone knew his post and duties in case of a night attack. He explained to the gathered officers that this might seem a rather unnecessary remark to make, but that, in view of the fact that ships' personnel were continually changing with varying escort requirements, a continuity in training was not easy to achieve. Outlining the course of action to be taken if the *Scharnhorst* should sortie, he stated that the prime objective was to close with the enemy and open fire with starshell, to illuminate the target at a range of 12000 yards. The four escorting destroyers of Force 2 would then form sub-divisions, and leave the battleship and cruiser to take up suitable positions for a torpedo attack. Finally, the *Jamaica* was to stay in close support of the *Duke of York*, but if heavily engaged, to break away and open the range. With the limited endurance of the destroyers (see table 2A) continuous cover could not be given to the convoy, he explained, and so Force 2 would sail to the area of Bear Island at 15 knots and be in the covering position when the convoy was just east of the island, allowing Force 2 to be in the dangerous area for about 30 hours.

Having outlined the plan of action Adm Fraser, together with Force 2, sailed from Akureyri at 23.00, at just about the same time as the escorts of JW 55B were being informed by the C-in-C Rosyth that the aircraft detailed for A/S duties for the convoy on the 24th would be a Catalina. Capt D 17 answered through SBNO North Russia at 23.15 giving the position of JW 55B at 01.00 for the 24th, its course, 037°, and a speed of 9 knots. He also reported the presence of shadowing aircraft which had been patrolling up and down the starboard side of the convoy and across the stern of it. A 20° wheel executed by the convoy at 20.00 had failed to lose the aircraft, which remained in contact until 23.05.

December 24th, 1943

During the early hours of December 24th, Force 2 carried out a final rehearsal for an attack on the *Scharnhorst* using the *Jamaica* as a target.

At 07.00 JW 55B commenced altering course to 057° in accordance with the convoy sailing instructions, completing the movement at 07.15, but was unable to shake off a shadowing aircraft which had found the convoy, and which remained in contact with it for the rest of the morning. The C-in-C Rosyth informed the escorts at 07.35 that the Catalina they were expecting as A/S escort was returning to its base, as flying conditions were unsuitable.

Daybreak showed the normally tidy columns of merchant ships scattered over a wide area, and at 11.30 the Commodore ordered the speed of the convoy to be reduced by one knot, to 7 knots (the convoy only managing to make 8 knots during the night), to enable the columns to close up to their normal positions, the *Haida*, meanwhile, taking on fuel from the *British Statesman*. The best speed the convoy could then make was $8\frac{1}{2}$ knots. At 12.00 the convoy was only 400 miles from Altenfiord, the base of the German naval squadron. Twenty-five minutes later the *Iroquois* reported two aircraft shadowing the convoy from astern, which were also sighted by a number of vessels in the port screen. Forces 1 and 2 were not in position to give close support to the convoy at 12.00 if the Germans should sortie, and there was only a light destroyer screen between them and the convoy. The Germans had not, however, penetrated so far west before, but after due deliberation Adm Fraser decided to break wireless silence, and at 13.25 ordered the convoy to reverse its course for three hours until 17.00. At the same time the speed of Force 2 was raised to 19 knots. The reversal of course of the convoy would mean that the *Scharnhorst* would be unable to locate the convoy until after dark, but this, and the increase in speed of Force 2, would not bring the two any closer together.

The speed of the convoy was again reduced to 8 knots at 13.40 to allow some of the stragglers to catch up. The *Haida* completed fuelling at 14.10, and fourteen minutes later the convoy increased speed by $\frac{1}{2}$ knot, and again at 14.30 to maintain a speed of advance of 9 knots.

Captain McCoy then received the signal sent by Adm Fraser, ordering him to reverse the course of the convoy for three hours until 17.00. Owing to the fact that the speed of the convoy had dropped below its scheduled rate of 9 knots during the night, and also that the Commodore had deliberately reduced speed during the morning to enable the scattered convoy to reassemble, it was calculated that by 17.00 JW 55B would be 20 miles behind its scheduled position. In the poor light the convoy was having difficulty in keeping station and the coloured lights that would have to be shown to turn the convoy round would clearly pinpoint its alteration of course to the shadowing aircraft. After consultation with the convoy Commodore it was felt that to reverse the course of the convoy would be impracticable, probably causing it to become more dispersed than it was already, and so the convoy Commodore and Capt D 17 decided to reduce the speed of JW 55B to 8 knots and to get it into order. This was done at 15.40 and it was felt that this move would have, under the circumstances mentioned above, the same effect as reversing the course of the convoy at 9 knots.

The usual daily report of the position, course and speed of the convoy was sent through SBNO North Russia at 18.00 by Capt McCoy, who also stated that the convoy had been shadowed from 12.20 until 16.26, when the aircraft lost touch with the convoy.

During the day Force 1 steered a course keeping to the south of RA 55A and turned to a northerly course at 19.00.

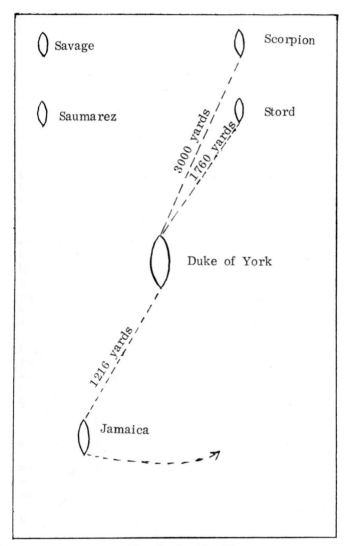

Fig. 1: The sailing disposition of Force 2

At 19.28 the *Honeysuckle*, on the starboard screen of JW 55B, fired two starshell, but it was a false alarm and she only succeeded in illuminating the *Wrestler*.

Christmas Day, December 25th, 1943

At 01.00 on the 25th, Force 1 altered course to 170°, and proceeded to zig-zag on north and south tracks for five hours at a time, over an area east of 25°. In the early hours Adm Fraser realised that JW 55B was not maintaining its proposed speed of $9\frac{1}{2}$ knots and that it would not pass RA 55A in the vicinity of Bear Island, as previously arranged. RA 55A was thus virtually without any heavy cover, and so the C-in-C diverted it to the north, away from any possible area of surface action. Together with this message, passed through the Rear-Adm (D) Home Fleet (Rear-Adm I. G. Glennie CB SNO Afloat Scapa Flow), he requested the SO in charge of the escort of RA 55A to detach four fleet destroyers to assist the escorts of JW 55B. The decision as to which destroyers was left to the SO in charge of RA 55A, Capt Campbell. The 36th Division was chosen as they had the largest reserves of fuel remaining and at 02.00 the four destroyers (*Musketeer* (SO), *Matchless*, *Opportune* and *Virago*) were detached from the convoy and ordered to rendezvous with JW 55B. Having sent these orders Adm Fraser then felt certain that the escorts of JW 55B and the cruisers of Force 1 would be able to force the *Scharnhorst* away from the convoy, possibly inflict some damage on her, and so give Force 2 time to close the battlecruiser.

During the morning the U-boat patrol line first made contact with JW 55B, *U-601* sighting the convoy at 09.01 in position 72° 32′ N–12° 30′ E, the *Whitehall* homing on to her sighting signal and reporting it at 10.04. A Do 18 shadowing aircraft was also sighted and reported at 11.15 by the *Iroquois*. Soon after being sighted the aircraft returned to its base owing to the worsening weather, the force 4 south-easterly wind increasing in strength to force 7 and veering to the south-west, and the squally rain showers turning to hard driving sleet. The *Whitehall* obtained a further U-boat bearing at 11.35 showing that the enemy forces were steadily building up for an attack on JW 55B. The atrocious weather conditions prevented the Germans from sending any further reconnaissance aircraft to shadow JW 55B during the 25th, but it was hoped that the U-boats now in contact would continue to shadow the convoy and report its movements. Owing to these movements, and changes of direction during the 24th, the course of the convoy was altered to 075° at 12.00 bringing it back to its scheduled route. The U-boat remained in contact during this alteration of course and a bearing on it at 12.09 showed that it was slowly moving up the port side of the convoy.

At 12.15 the Battle Group was ordered by Rear-Adm Kluber, Flag Officer Navy (North Norway), to come to one hour's notice for steaming. Events were beginning to gather pace as the Germans prepared to sortie against JW 55B.

The *Orwell* and *Whitehall* escorting JW 55B were sent to investigate an HF/DF bearing of 208°—*U-601*—on the port side of the convoy at 12.35, being ordered to sweep to a depth of 10 miles from the convoy. While they were away the 36th Division detached from RA 55A joined the escort at 12.55 and took up station 4 miles ahead of the convoy, the destroyers spaced one mile apart. While sweeping to gain a contact on *U-601* the *Whitehall* gained a second HF/DF at 12.58 on a bearing of 260°.

Operation Eastern Front commences, December 25th, 1943

Adm Doenitz finally sent the signal ordering the start of operations against JW 55B by the Battle Group at 14.15, the signal reading "Eastern Front—17.00". This signified that the Battle Group was to sail at 17.00. The orders sent to Adm Schneiwind by Adm Doenitz were quite explicit as to the conduct of the operations by Rear-Adm Bey. They stated that as the enemy was trying to assist the Russian armies on the Eastern Front by sending them supplies and weapons, the German Navy ought to try and help its armies fighting the Russians. To this end the *Scharnhorst* and the five destroyers of Battle Group 1 (*Z29*, *Z30*, *Z33*, *Z34* and *Z38*) would sortie and attack the convoy. If, however, certain conditions arose the action could be broken off, at the discretion of Navy Group North. These conditions were, that if strong enemy forces appeared the *Scharnhorst* was to disengage. At 14.20 *U-601* sent a further sighting report of JW 55B giving the position of the convoy and a weather report, which showed conditions slowly deteriorating. The wind was now blowing from the south at force 7 with heavy rain, and the visibility was down to two miles. These worsening conditions, and the fact that no air reconnaissance was possible, led Adm Schneiwind to ask Adm Doenitz for a postponement of the operation. He proposed a new plan whereby the destroyers would attack the convoy while the *Scharnhorst* covered them at a distance. Adm Doenitz refused to alter his original plan, which intended that the *Scharnhorst* would attack the convoy in the approximate longitude of North Cape during the night. Three of the destroyers would shadow the convoy until daylight when the *Scharnhorst* and the other two destroyers that had been standing off in the dark would close and attack the convoy at close quarters. If heavy enemy ships appeared the *Scharnhorst* would immediately disengage and her withdrawal would be covered by the destroyers fighting a delaying action.

An hour after the initial order was sent, at 15.15, Adm Schneiwind passed on the order—Operation Eastern Front 17.00—to Rear-Adm Bey. Adm Bey's orders were to take the *Scharnhorst* and five destroyers and attack the convoy at first light on the 26th—about 10.00—and to attack only if the weather and visibility were suitable, and if he had sufficient information regarding the enemy's forces. If conditions were unfavourable to the *Scharnhorst*, the destroyers would attack the convoy on their own while the *Scharnhorst* would stand off at a distance, or await events in one of the outer fiords on the Norwegian coast.

As he did not receive the order to commence operations until late in the afternoon Rear-Adm Bey had to put forward the time of sailing from 17.00 to 19.00, in order to give himself enough time to transfer his flag and staff of 30 from the *Tirpitz* to the *Scharnhorst*. At the same time he called a conference of the CO's of the ships involved on board the *Tirpitz*.

U-boats report the convoy

Following the earlier contacts with the U-boats nothing more was heard until 15.42 when *U-601* was heard transmitting a message either astern or on the port quarter of the convoy. She reported the escorts to JW 55B as consisting of three cruisers, five destroyers and four smaller vessels, but stated that no heavier forces had been sighted. The *Orwell* and *Whitehall* returned to the convoy at 17.00 having had no success in searching for the U-boats, but soon after, at 17.48, the *Onslow* and *Whitehall* gained further HF/DF contacts on a second U-boat bearing 060°. A fix from the *Onslow*, *Whitehall* and *Wrestler* at 18.24 indicated that this U-boat was about 20 miles astern of the convoy and shadowing it.

At 19.00 the *Scharnhorst* and the destroyers Z29, Z34, and Z38 preceded by three minesweepers left Altenfiord (see fig. 4) heading for the navigational point Lucie. This point was several miles west of the mouth of the fiord and on reaching the point the minesweepers would leave the Battle Group which would then proceed on a course to intercept the convoy. At Kaa Fiord the Battle Group was joined by the destroyers *Z30* and *Z33*. Under command of Rear-Adm Bey (the Adm commanding destroyers) replacing Adm Kummetz who was on leave, and captained by Capt Hintze who was on his first operational sortie in the battlecruiser, the *Scharnhorst* headed for the open sea. On board were 40 cadets taking the place of regular officers away on leave and having their first training cruise of the war.

Just before 20.00 *U-716* received a message from the Cdre U-boats in Norway ordering all the boats in Group Eisenbart to attack JW 55B, if sighted, whatever the weather. Almost as soon as it surfaced *U-716* sighted a destroyer and fired a torpedo at it which passed ahead. At 20.30 JW 55B was due to alter its course for the night by 20°, but the weather conditions (wind force 8 from the SSE) forced the Cdre to request a postponement of this from Capt D 17 and to allow the convoy to stay on its present course. To turn the convoy in the weather conditions then encountered would have endangered the deck cargoes possibly shifting them from their moorings and the ships' boats might well get smashed as well. Capt McCoy agreed to stay on the present course until 10.00 the following day.

By 21.16 Battle Group 1 was steaming north at 25 knots and was only a few hours' steaming from the convoy. The severe weather conditions, high winds and heavy seas were making the destroyers almost unmanageable, and Rear-Adm Bey made a signal to Group Command North stating the situation. Steering was extremely difficult and the guns on the destroyers were unuseable. At 23.00 the *Scharnhorst* altered course to 010° and not long after Rear-Adm Bey received a signal from Adm Doenitz. The signal read:

1. A convoy to Russia is sending materials to be used against our troops on the eastern front. We must come to their aid.

2. The convoy is to be attacked by the *Scharnhorst* and the destroyers.

3. The tactical situation must be exploited with skill and daring and the attack must not end in stalemate. Every opportunity to attack must be seized using the *Scharnhorst*'s superiority to the best advantage. The destroyers are to be used later.

4. You may use your own judgement as to when to break off action. You must disengage if a superior enemy is encountered.
5. Inform all the crews accordingly. I have full confidence in your offensive spirit.

At 23.55 Rear-Adm Bey broke wireless silence again and sent a signal to Navy Group North informing them that he was probably in the operation area, and that the firepower of his destroyers was seriously impaired and that speed had had to be reduced.

Force 2 meanwhile was maintaining its eastward course at 17 knots. The heavy seas that were running, however, were making conditions most unpleasant on board the British ships too. Even on board the *Duke of York* few people managed to get any sleep and large quantities of water were shipped down the ventilation trunking.

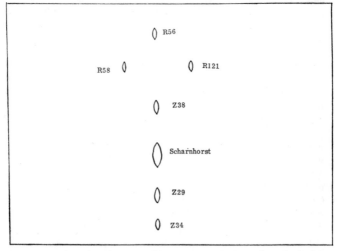

Fig. 4: The sailing disposition of the German Battle Group down the fiord

CHAPTER TWO

The forces converge

Rear-Adm Bey was steaming on a northerly course of 012° at 25 knots when at 00.28 he received a signal informing him that the Luftwaffe had reported that they had lost contact with the convoy at 16.25 on the previous day. The signal, however, gave no position of the convoy. At 00.58 Rear-Adm Bey received a second signal to the effect that a B & V 138 flying boat had last sighted JW 55B at 15.10 the previous day, and that a radar search had failed to contact any enemy forces within a distance of 50 miles. There was still no report of the convoy's position, however.

It was Vice-Adm Burnett's intention to be in a position about 40 miles east of JW 55B at 08.00 on the 26th. In order to arrive in this position he altered course to 260° at 01.00. The ether was now becoming thick with signals as the forces converged. At 02.14 Rear-Adm Bey received a further signal from Group Command North, which was a relay of the signal sent to them at 21.16 the previous evening by Adm Doenitz. In addition to Adm Doenitz's message, Group Command North stressed that if the *Scharnhorst* were to attack the convoy on her own, this would involve her in serious risks, but any final decision as to whether or not to attack was to be left to Rear-Adm Bey. The sailing of the German Battle Group from the Norwegian fiord had been observed, and the Admiralty received a report of this in the early hours of the 26th. At 03.19 the Admiralty sent Adm Fraser a message, which he received twenty minutes later, informing him that the *Scharnhorst* had sailed. The one fear in Adm Fraser's mind at this moment was that if the *Scharnhorst* attacked the convoy at daylight and retired at once, he was too far away to be of any assistance.

Because JW 55B had been more or less continually shadowed by aircraft since leaving Iceland, and as U-boats had also gained contact with the convoy, it was fairly obvious that this was to be the *Scharnhorst*'s quarry, especially as RA 55A was still undetected. At

04.00 RA 55A was about 200 miles west of Beard Islan, steering a course of 267° at 8 knots. South of Bear Island at a distance of 50 miles, JW 55B was steering a course of 070° also at 8 knots. The *Belfast* with Force 1 was on a course of 235° steaming at 18 knots 150 miles east of JW 55B, while 350 miles to the south-west Force 2 was steaming at 24 knots—its best speed in the foul weather—on a course of 080°, to catch up with the convoy and Force 1 (see fig. 3). The strong south-westerly wind of force 7 was, however, causing much trouble to Force 2, causing it to keep its speed down in an effort to prevent the destroyers broaching to in the heavy following sea. The *Duke of York* was not immune to the weather either, her bows being continually submerged, and much water finding its way down the ventilation trunking.

In a signal timed 04.01, ordering Capt D 17 to turn convoy JW 55B on to a northerly course and asking Vice-Adm Burnett to report his position, Adm Fraser gave his own position, course and speed (71° 07′ N–10° 48′ E, 080°, 24 knots), breaking wireless silence for a second time. At 05.46 Vice-Adm Burnett replied to Adm Fraser's signal giving the position, course and speed of Force 1 (73° 38′ N–26° 00′ E, 235°, 18 knots). The seas were now extremely rough, with a leaden sky and the wind blowing a strong gale from the south-west, force 7 to 8.

Just before 06.00 the weather began to improve slightly and the

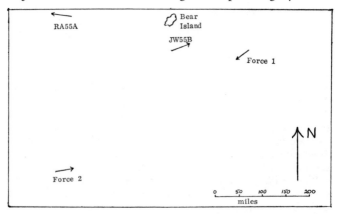

Fig. 3: The situation 04.00 hrs.

ABOVE: Vice-Admiral Sir Bruce Austin Fraser, KBE, CBE, on his appointment as C-in-C of the Home Fleet. BELOW: A convoy zig-zagging its way across the Atlantic.   [Imperial War Museum

The Convoy

[*Imperial War Museum*

The Convoy Conference

[*Imperial War Museum*

The Convoy sets sail   [*Imperial War Museum*

HMS Belfast *in Northern waters.*   [*Imperial War Museum*

ABOVE: HMS Whitehall: *note hedgehog in "A" position, radar at top of foremast and extra-light AA.* BELOW: HMCS Iroquois. *FACING PAGE: HMS* Orwell. [*Imperial War Museum*

ABOVE: A King George V Class battle-ship firing "Y" turret 14in guns.
BELOW: HMS Honeysuckle.

ABOVE: An Arctic convoy: note men chipping away ice in the bows. BELOW: Admiral Schniewind (centre). [Imperial War Museum

ABOVE: *HMS* Duke of York *in heavy seas.* BELOW: *A conference in the chartroom of the Scharnhorst.* FACING PAGE: Scharnhorst *in Arctic waters.*

[*Imperial War Museum*

TOP: Z29 *in a Norwegian Fiord.*
ABOVE: Z38.   [*Druppel : Real Photos*

TOP: HMS Sheffield.   ABOVE: *Radar operator: he passes the range and bearing through the voice tube by his head.*

[Imperial War Museum

FACING PAGE: Rear Amiral R. L. Burnett, CB, OBE, DSO in his cabin on board HMS Belfast. ABOVE: Inside a 6 in. turret: the crew, wearing respirators and anti-flash clothing, are ramming home a shell. BELOW: Interior of an 8 in. turret.

[Imperial War Museum

ABOVE: The engine room of a cruiser, showing controls and telegraph. BELOW: Part of the engine room of a cruiser.

[*Imperial War Museum*

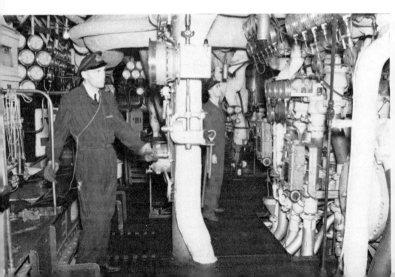

ABOVE: *The 6 in. turret of HMS* Jamaica.
BELOW: *HMS* Duke of York *firing her 5.25 in. guns.* [*Imperial War Museum*

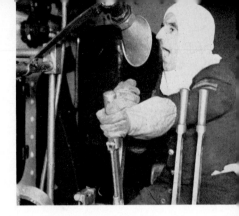

ABOVE: The captain of a 14 in. turret on HMS Duke of York replying through the voice tube to the working chamber while operating the cage control levers. BELOW: A 4.7 in. gun crew on a destroyer.

[*Imperial War Museum*

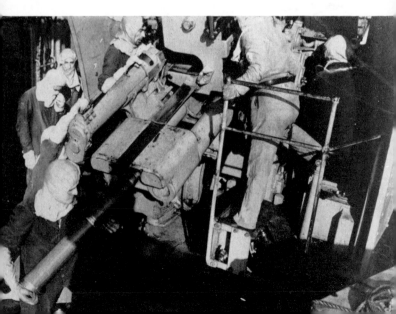

36th Destroyer Division began a sweep down the starboard side of the convoy to a depth of 15 miles to put down *U-716* which was shadowing the convoy. Five minutes later, at 06.05, the *Onslow* received the C-in-C's signal ordering JW 55B to steer to the north, and it conformed immediately, altering course by 20° wheels. A further signal ordering the convoy to steer a course of 045° was sent by the C-in-C at 06.28 and at the same time Force 1 was ordered to close the convoy and give it close cover.

The *Belfast* was brought to a state of First Degree Readiness at 07.00, just as the *Scharnhorst* was ordering the 4th Destroyer Flotilla to commence a reconnaissance across the estimated course of JW 55B. Rear-Adm Bey ordered the Battle Group to steer a course of 250° at a speed of 12 knots and the *Scharnhorst* turned away to the south-west. In the mountainous seas and high headwind the German destroyers were hard put to keep on the course ordered by Rear-Adm Bey and they had to reduce speed to 10 knots.

The C-in-C's signal of 06.28 was received by the *Onslow* at 07.05, just as the convoy had reached a new course of 035°. The 06.28 signal was received by Force 1 at 06.51 and at 07.12 the squadron changed on to a new course of 270° and approached the convoy from the south-west, thus avoiding the possibility of having to steam into the heavy seas if action should occur.

By 07.30 Rear-Adm Bey estimated that he was 40 miles south-east of Bear Island in position 73° 52′ N–23° 10′ E and he ordered the crew of *Scharnhorst* to action stations. The *Scharnhorst* signalled an alteration of course to 230° at 07.55 at the same time turning the battlecruiser from her south-westerly course on to a course north of west. The 4th Destroyer Flotilla was ordered to form a patrol line 5 miles apart at a distance of 10 miles ahead of the *Scharnhorst*. Unfortunately the destroyers only received part of the signal and they and the *Scharnhorst* unintentionally parted company, the destroyers patrolling an area which was not the one that Rear-Adm Bey had intended they should cover.

Following a report of JW 55B's position, course and speed received at 07.42, Force 1 altered course to 300° at 08.00 in order to converge with the convoy, as requested by the C-in-C. There was, however, an error in the signal and a correction to the convoy's position was given to Vice-Adm Burnett just after 08.00. Meanwhile the 36th Destroyer Division completed its sweep for *U-716*, passing over the submarine in position 73° 00′ N–17° 25′ E and returning to the escort of JW 55B at 08.14. As soon as the destroyers had passed overhead *U–716* surfaced and made a sighting report which was received in the *Scharnhorst* causing her to alter course to the north-east. At this point all communication between the *Scharnhorst* and the 4th Destroyer Flotilla ceased.

Having received the signal giving a correction to JW 55B's position, Vice-Adm Burnett altered the course of Force 1 another 5° at 08.15 bringing the squadron on to a course of 305° and increasing the speed of the cruisers to 24 knots.

The Scharnhorst detected

At 08.30 the *Sheffield* was brought to a state of First Degree Readiness and four minutes later the Type 273 radar in *Norfolk* picked up the *Scharnhorst* on a bearing of 280° at a distance of 33000 yards. This was followed at 08.40 by the Type 273 in the *Belfast* gaining a contact bearing 295° at 35000 yards range, to which the cruiser locked her 6″ guns (see fig. 5). Vice-Adm Burnett immediately sent off a report of the radar contact which was heard by Capt McCoy in the *Onslow* at 08.44. Just before the *Belfast* gained radar contact, at 08.39, Capt McCoy ordered the 36th Destroyer Division to take up station six miles ahead of JW 55B spacing the destroyers one mile apart on a bearing of 165° from the convoy. At 08.50 the *Sheffield* gained radar contact with the target, her Type 273 giving an echo bearing 278° at a distance of 30500 yards.

Five minutes later Capt Johannesson in the *Z29* sent off an enemy sighting report, at the same time ordering *Z29* and *Z30* to prepare to fire at a target the German destroyer had detected. Almost at once, however, he realised he had made a mistake—the destroyer he was about to fire on being *Z38* who was out of position to the north. Unknown to the 4th Flotilla the *Scharnhorst* had meantime made a 360° turn at 08.49 and continued on her original course.

While the British forces were closing in on the *Scharnhorst* the Russian C-in-C, Adm A. G. Golovko, ordered the submarines *L20* (Capt V. F. Tamman), *K21* (Capt Z. M. Arvanov) and *S102* (Capt L. I. Gorodshedshev) to the area of North Cape to intercept the battlecruiser, if possible, and to attack only if it was certain that the vessel intercepted was the *Scharnhorst*. At the same time destroyers at the main base of the Fleet raised steam in preparation to sail and aircraft were armed with bombs and torpedoes.

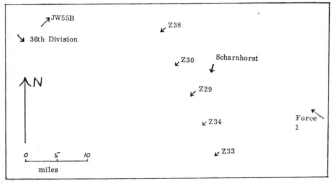

Fig. 5: The situation 08.40

The first action

At 09.00 the Type 273 on the *Belfast* picked up a second echo bearing 299° at a range of 24500 yards. Three minutes later the 6″ armament of the *Belfast* was trained on the new echo (bearing 298°, 23000 yards). The three cruisers formed a line of bearing of 180° to the first echo at 09.04, and four minutes later the range of the second echo was down to 20500 yards on a bearing of 283° from the *Sheffield*. Confirmation of the bearing of the *Scharnhorst* from the convoy of 125° at a distance of 35 miles was received by Capt McCoy at 09.12 and was substantiated by a radar report. At 09.15 Force 1 altered course to 160° with the *Belfast* leading and retraining her 6″ armament to the original echo. She was followed by the *Sheffield*, while the *Norfolk* brought up the rear. At this point the *Scharnhorst* appeared to be moving along a course of 070° at 18 knots at a distance of 13000 yards, bearing 250° from Force 1. The *Sheffield* was the first to sight the battlecruiser, on a bearing of 222° at 09.21, when the range was 13000 yards. The *Belfast* opened fire at 09.24 with starshell, but failed to illuminate the target and so the *Norfolk* followed suit a minute later with her non-flashless cordite. (At this point in her career the *Norfolk* had not been equipped with the flashless cordite as were the other cruisers.) These bursting starshell were seen from the *Onslow* on a bearing of 129° and were followed by a number of gun flashes. The *Scharnhorst* was still, however, out of range of the starshell and

35

the *Belfast* and *Norfolk* withheld their fire. The *Sheffield* made the next attempt to illuminate the battlecruiser, firing five salvoes of starshell at 09.29 at a range of 11700 yards on a bearing of 185°. The target still remained outside the effective range of the starshell, and so the *Sheffield* too withheld fire. This was too much, and Vice-Adm Burnett ordered the cruisers to open fire at 09.29, to which the *Norfolk* complied at 09.30 firing six broadsides of high explosive at a range of 9800 yards, when all her turrets were bearing. She employed the blind fire technique using radar ranges and bearings. It was also decided to ignore the second echo as it was thought that from its speed of about 8 to 10 knots that it must be a merchant ship. It was in fact *Z38* which was out of position with the rest of the German 4th Destroyer Flotilla.

With the battle in full swing Adm Fraser ordered Capt McCoy to turn JW 55B on to a northerly course to clear the battle area, to which Capt McCoy complied at 09.30. At 09.30 the three cruisers of Force 1 altered course to 265° but only the *Norfolk* opened fire at the *Scharnhorst*, as she was now masking the turrets of *Belfast* and *Sheffield*. Almost immediately the *Norfolk* dropped back to clear the *Belfast*, at the same time claiming hits on the *Scharnhorst* with her second or third salvoes. These hits landed on the port high angle director abreast the bridge controlling the forward portside 5.9″ guns, putting it out of action and destroying the radar aerial atop the bridge. Another shell penetrated the fo'c'sle deck, finishing up in the crew's quarters, and a third landed between the third 5.9″ turret on the portside and the torpedo tubes. These hits were confirmed by the *Belfast*. At 09.35 Capt McCoy signalled to Vice-Adm Burnett asking him if he required the assistance of any destroyers. Two minutes later Adm Fraser ordered Capt McCoy to send four destroyers to the assistance of Force 1. Vice-Adm Burnett had no knowledge of this signal from Adm Fraser, and after receiving Capt McCoy's initial signal offering assistance Vice-Adm Burnett replied requesting the assistance of six destroyers.

The *Scharnhorst* retires

To conform to the *Scharnhorst*'s alteration of course to about 150° Force 1 altered course to 105° at 09.38 and as the *Scharnhorst* worked up to a speed of 30 knots the range rapidly opened. Meanwhile the *Scharnhorst* fired a number of blind salvoes with her after turret. With the range opening, Force 1 worked up to its maximum speed of 24 knots in the force 7 to 8 south-westerly gale, and two minutes later at 09.40 the *Norfolk* ceased fire.

As the *Norfolk* ceased fire the *Whitehall* in the convoy escort obtained an HF/DF submarine contact on a bearing of 014° and together with the *Wrestler* was ordered to search for the U-boat to a depth of 15 miles. While the two destroyers were away searching for the U-boat the 36th Destroyer Division formed up in line ahead with the *Musketeer* in the lead at 09.45 and steadied on a course of 045° steaming at 9 knots. They were six miles from JW 55B on a bearing of 165° from the convoy.

Just as the 36th Division was forming up in line ahead Rear-Adm Bey received a sighting report of the convoy from *U-277* which placed JW 55B in position 73° 58′ N–19° 30′ E. Rear-Adm Bey, however, ignored the sighting report and continued on his original course.

By 09.46 the distance between Force 1 and the *Scharnhorst* had increased to 24000 yards and was still increasing as the *Scharnhorst* continued to steam on at 30 knots altering course to 150°. As she altered course Rear-Adm Bey signalled to Adm Doenitz that he was being engaged by a cruiser using radar directed gunnery. To conform to the *Scharnhorst*'s movement Force 1 altered course to 170°.

Following Adm Fraser's order of 09.37 Capt McCoy detached the

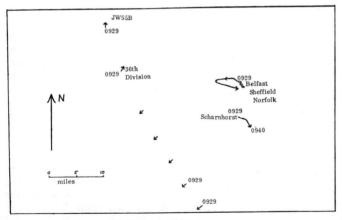

Fig. 6: The situation 09.30–09.40

four destroyers of the 36th Division at 09.51 with orders to join Force 1. The destroyers then shaped course to 120° and increased speed to 22 knots to catch the cruisers.

Although the action between the cruisers and *Scharnhorst* had ceased, the battlecruiser had still not given up the idea of attacking JW 55B, and at 09.55 she turned to a north-easterly course in an attempt to work round the convoy and attack it from the north. Force 1 at once changed course to 150° and five minutes later at 10.00 altered to 305° to get between the convoy and the *Scharnhorst*.

At 10.09 the German 4th Destroyer Flotilla received an order to "advance into the immediate vicinity of the convoy" but Capt Johannesson replied that he was proceeding on a course of 230° at 12 knots, as last ordered. About this time three German B &V 138 reconnaissance aircraft gained radar contact with Force 2 and began to shadow it from the starboard three-quarter reporting the force as several unidentified vessels, one large one and several small, in position 72° 07′ N–21° 05′ E at 10.12. The position given, however, was 49 miles ENE of Adm Fraser's true position. Force 1 altered course to 325° at 10.14 and five minutes later the echo of the *Scharnhorst* disappeared off the radar screen of *Belfast*, the last radar report showing that the battlecruiser was still steaming at about 30 knots in a north-easterly direction at a range of 36000 yards and on a bearing of 078°.

The cruisers cover JW 55B

Six minutes after losing contact with the *Scharnhorst*, at 10.25, the 36th Division detached from JW 55B was identified on the radar plot of *Sheffield*, bearing 299° at a range of 17600 yards and closing rapidly. The German destroyers were also being given orders, at 10.27 being told to steer a course of 070° and to increase speed to 25 knots by Rear-Adm Bey. At 10.30 the *Musketeer* sighted Force 1 at a distance of 4 miles on a bearing of 110°, and received the order to station the 36th Division in a screen ahead of Force 1 at a speed of 28 knots. At this point Capt McCoy escorting JW 55B was informed that Vice-Adm Burnett had lost touch with the *Scharnhorst* and so he ordered the Cdre to alter the course of JW 55B back to 045° which movement was completed at 10.44.

At 10.45, Force 1 was in position 73° 49′ N–21° 58′ E and five minutes later the radar detected JW 55B on a bearing of 324° at a range of 28000 yards. Vice-Adm Burnett then proceeded to patrol on a zig-zag route at 28 knots at a distance of 10 miles in front of the convoy. On reaching the position for the second leg of the zig-zag, at 10.54, the 36th Division endeavoured to conform to the 10° alteration of course to starboard but the following wind and high seas caused the vessels to yaw and roll so violently that the *Opportune* became unmanageable. The same problem was encountered again at 10.58 when JW 55B was at a distance of 27000 yards from the *Sheffield* on a bearing of 322°. Ten minutes afterwards, at 11.08, the problems of steering the destroyers were such that Vice-Adm Burnett was forced to alter course to 000° and reduce speed to 18 knots. The destroyers then closed the cruisers and formed an anti-submarine screen round them at 11.10, at 11.21 taking station on a course of 045°.

At 11.22 the *Musketeer* detected an aircraft at a distance of $21\frac{1}{2}$ miles on a bearing of 073°. Three minutes later the aircraft was on a bearing of 080° 21 miles away and by 11.26 had closed to 19 miles on a bearing of 095°. At 11.35 the *Norfolk*'s surface warning radar picked up a contact at a range of 27000 yards bearing 127°. Vice-Adm Burnett reported it to Scapa Flow at 11.43 as an unidentified vessel, course 140°, bearing 149°, range 12 miles. The echo, however, was lost a few minutes later at 11.50.

By this time the fuel in the destroyers escorting Force 2 was running low and Adm Fraser had to make the agonising decision of whether he should carry on to try and catch the *Scharnhorst*, if Force 1 regained contact with her, or return to Scapa Flow.

The second action

At 11.55 Force 1 was steering a course of 045° at 18 knots as the convoy commenced a wheel to 125° in order to place Force 1 between JW 55B and the *Scharnhorst*. This followed a signal received by Capt McCoy from Adm Fraser at 11.22 telling him to use his discretion as to what course the convoy should steer. At 11.58 Rear-Adm Bey ordered the 4th Destroyer Flotilla to attack JW 55B in the position given by *U-277* at 09.45. The destroyers were now well to the east of the convoy, and to reach the position given had to turn round and head into the wind again. Seven minutes later at 12.05 the Type 273 radar placed the convoy 9 miles from Force 1 on its port quarter on a bearing of 275°. At this point the 36th Division, with *Musketeer* in the lead, was ordered to concentrate on the starboard bow of Force 1, which they did at 12.07, forming up in line ahead, one mile in front of the *Belfast*, on a course of 045° at a speed of 18 knots. A minute later they were ordered to take station on a bearing of 090° from the *Belfast* at a distance of two miles. At 12.10 the Type 273 on the *Sheffield* picked up a contact bearing 079° at a distance of 27000 yards. The echo was held at 12.15 and the two wing Type 285 used to sweep the area. With the target appearing to steer a course of 240° Force 1 altered course to 100°. Vice-Adm Burnett ordered the cruisers to open fire when the range was down to 11500 yards, and at 12.20 ordered the 36th Division to try and close

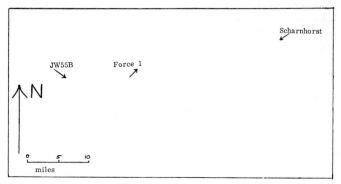

Fig. 7: The situation 12.05

the *Scharnhorst* and attack her with torpedoes. By 12.23 the range of the echo was down to 13000 yards and closing rapidly and the 6″ guns of the *Sheffield* were brought to the ready. The *Belfast* then fired starshell when the range was 10500 yards, which was observed from JW 55B on a bearing of 083°. All three cruisers commenced firing full broadsides at the target which was in sight at 12.24, the *Musketeer* following suit when the *Scharnhorst* was 7000 yards from the 36th Division. As soon as fire was opened the *Scharnhorst* turned to the north-west and opened fire on Force 1 which changed course to 040°. Three of these salvoes straddled the port and starboard quarter of the rear ship of the 36th Division—the *Virago*—which had just passed ahead of Force 1 as fire was opened. The shells from these salvoes fell between 400 and 1000 yards from the destroyer. As soon as he saw the gunflashes, Capt McCoy ordered the Fleet destroyer escort of JW 55B to form a protective screen by divisions on the port side of the convoy in case the *Scharnhorst* should evade Force 1 and attack the convoy.

For the first three minutes of the action the *Sheffield* and the *Belfast* fired full broadsides, the *Sheffield* getting off five and the *Belfast* nine 12 gun salvoes, using radar ranges and bearings. Hits on the *Scharnhorst* were observed from the *Sheffield*'s second broadside and the *Belfast*'s fourth. The range slowly opened, increasing from 8000 to 12500 yards.

On the *Norfolk*, only A and B turrets were bearing and they managed to fire ten broadsides, of which seven were considered hits, before a shell from the *Scharnhorst* hit the barbette of X turret at 12.27, putting it out of action. A shell also landed amidships on the *Norfolk*. The Type 284 radar set was put out of action by these hits, the Type 273 set damaged, and all other sets rendered unserviceable. In addition one officer and six ratings were killed and five ratings seriously wounded. Following the two explosions B turret fired four more salvoes using the last ranges fed from the Type 284 before fire was temporarily checked.

While the *Norfolk* was receiving most of the *Scharnhorst's* fire, a salvo from the battlecruiser also straddled the *Sheffield*. A number of shell splinters penetrated the cruiser, but caused no serious damage. At the same time as the *Norfolk* was being hit, an error in the orders from the Fire Control Officer on the *Sheffield* led to a reduction in the volume of fire from the cruiser. Due to the bad visibility and the difficulty of seeing the target owing to the heavy spray and cordite smoke, salvoes were ordered to be fired instead of the broadsides, which would normally have been ordered to replace the rapid broadsides originally ordered. This reduced fire from the *Sheffield* continued for the next seven minutes, before the order for salvoes was countermanded. Fire from the *Sheffield* was finally checked at 12.40 when the target had disappeared out of visual sight at a range of 11400 yards.

Following the nine full broadsides fired from the *Belfast*, A and B turrets continued firing broadsides, as X and Y turrets could not bear. Between them A and B turrets then fired eight salvoes using the visual technique before resorting to the blind fire method for a further eight salvoes, from which hits on the target were observed from the fifth salvo. After this the Type 284 radar set developed a fault, and was unable to give a steady echo from the target. The Type 273 was then used and the best information from this used to fire a few more salvoes, fire being checked at 12.41 when the range had opened to 12400 yards.

On the *Norfolk* the Type 284 radar set was soon repaired but great difficulty was then found in holding the target with the aerial, due to the rapid alterations of course made by the cruiser in an attempt to avoid the fire from the *Scharnhorst*. The *Scharnhorst* was finding the *Norfolk* a much easier target to range on to due to the cruiser not having been equipped with flashless cordite. After a while reasonable readings were obtained from the Type 284 set and a further nine broadsides fired before fire was finally checked.

During the action the *Scharnhorst* made frequent alterations of course, at 12.28 hauling round on a course to port while Force 1 conformed, by altering to 090° at a distance of 9000 yards. By 12.30 the battlecruiser had altered to a course of 135° on a bearing of 113° from Force 1 which then increased speed to 28 knots. The *Scharnhorst* continued steaming at 18 knots at a distance of 10400 yards from Force 1 and, at 12.31, the 36th Division had to increase speed to 26 knots in their attempt to catch the battlecruiser. At 12.35 they altered course to 135° to conform to the *Scharnhorst*'s movements. The battlecruiser then altered course again, to 110°, and began to forge ahead of Force 1 as she worked up to a speed of 28 knots. The *Musketeer* ceased fire at 12.36 after expending about 52 salvoes, and was followed by the *Virago* opening fire a minute later with A, B and X turrets. At 12.41 when the cruiser action ceased, the 36th Division increased speed to 28 knots to chase the *Scharnhorst*, the *Virago* having fired six salvoes before checking at 12.47.

As the action ceased at 12.41 Force 1 commenced shadowing, and at 12.46 came up with the 36th Division, still endeavouring to catch up with the *Scharnhorst*. The destroyers were approached from the port quarter, the cruisers steaming in line abreast in the order left to right—*Belfast*, *Sheffield* and *Norfolk*. The 36th Division took station on the *Norfolk*'s starboard bow at a distance of one mile, the Force steaming a mean course of 110° at 28 knots. By 12.50 the range had opened to 13400 yards and the battlecruiser was on a bearing of 138°.

The chase

By 13.00 it was clear that the second action was over, the *Scharnhorst* having broken away and being chased by Force 1. With the immediate danger over, Capt McCoy ordered the Fleet destroyers of JW 55B to redispose themselves as an A/S screen round the convoy.

At 13.06 the report of the reconnaissance aircraft which had shadowed Force 2 during the morning was relayed by the Air Commander Lofoten to Rear-Adm Bey, but the signal omitted to make any mention of the large ship. About 14.00 the shadowing aircraft lost touch with the *Duke of York* and Adm Fraser received no more messages of the aircraft reporting the position of Force 2.

The cruisers of Force 1, spaced 1600 yards apart, continued to shadow the *Scharnhorst* for three hours following the second action, tracking the battlecruiser by radar at a distance of $7\frac{1}{2}$ miles (just outside the range of visibility of 7 miles). The Force kept to a tight formation in order not to confuse the radar screen with a number of echoes, and conformed to the *Scharnhorst*'s movements to the south and south-east, by making several 10° wheels to port. As a result of these movements the *Musketeer*, which had been steaming at 32 knots since 14.18, found herself abaft the beam of *Norfolk*, the starboard wing cruiser. Heading into the high seas the destroyers frequently shipped large quantities of water over their starboard bows.

The German destroyers of the 4th Flotilla had concentrated on the most northerly destroyer—*Z38*—and were steering a westerly course in search of the convoy, passing about 8 miles to the south of it at 13.00. At 14.18 Capt Johannesson received a signal from Rear-Adm Bey ordering him to break off action. Capt Johannesson queried the order but at 14.20 was ordered to return to base, which he did at a speed of 12 knots. Rear-Adm Bey then signalled Group North at 15.25 giving them his estimated time of arrival back at the base.

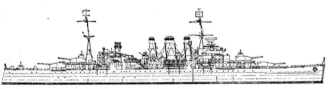

HMS Norfolk

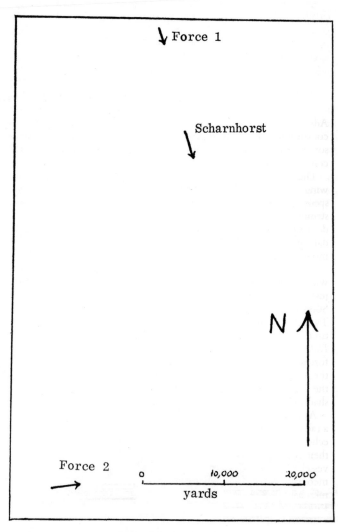

Force 1

Scharnhorst

N

Force 2

| 0 | 10,000 | 20,000 |

yards

Fig. 8: The situation 16.17

CHAPTER THREE

Force 2 detects the Scharnhorst

Adm Fraser now knew that if the *Scharnhorst* maintained her present course and speed, action would be joined about 17.15, unless of course something unforeseen should occur, such as Force 1 losing radar contact with the battlecruiser.

The *Norfolk* was forced to reduce speed at 16.03 to fight a fire in a wing compartment and seven minutes later the *Sheffield* reduced speed to 8 knots, reporting that her port inner shaft bearing had stripped. In order to prevent the excessive vibration thus caused from damaging the other shafts, speed had to be reduced, to lock the damaged shaft. As the *Sheffield* dropped back, the 36th Division moved over in line ahead to the starboard flank of the *Belfast*.

The convoy, meanwhile, continued to be shadowed by U-boats, who hourly reported its position. At 16.00 it altered course to 105° just about the same time as the *Scharnhorst* altered course to the south. Soon after she altered course, the battlecruiser was detected by the Type 273 radar on the *Duke of York*, at a range of 45500 yards. The time was 16.17 and the *Scharnhorst* was on a bearing of 020° from the *Duke of York* zig-zagging on a mean course of 160°. The opposing forces approached each other rapidly, the remaining radar set aft in the *Scharnhorst* failing to pick up Force 2. Not long after picking up the German battlecruiser on the radar plot, Force 1 was picked up, shadowing the *Scharnhorst*.

At 16.20 the *Musketeer*, leading the 36th Division at 30 knots, made a radar contact at 15000 yards on a bearing of 196°. The course of the echo slowly converged on that of the destroyers, who maintained their course and speed in order not to lose ground on Force 1. The vessel was sighted at a distance of 3000 yards, and identified as the merchant ship *Ocean Etapy*, when at a distance of 1500 yards. The merchant ship was steering an easterly course, and the *Opportune* and *Virago* altered course slightly to avoid her.

By 16.21 the *Sheffield* had managed to lock her damaged shaft and was working up to a maximum speed of 23 knots. The *Belfast*, however, was by now $4\frac{1}{2}$ miles ahead, steaming at a steady 27 knots, and all the *Sheffield* could do was to follow at her best speed. At 16.25 the *Norfolk* picked up a radar contact at a distance of $4\frac{1}{2}$ miles, bearing 212°. This echo turned out to be the merchant ship previously identified by the 36th Division.

The *Duke of York* was now slowly closing up on the *Scharnhorst* and at 16.32 the Type 284 gunnery control radar on the battleship homed on to the target at a range of 29700 yards. This occurred just as the CO of the *Savage* was ordering the destroyers to close up on their sub-division leaders, the *Savage* and *Saumarez* on the port bow of the *Duke of York* and the *Scorpion* and *Stord* on the starboard bow (see fig. 9). A minute later at 16.33 the Type 272 radar on the *Jamaica* homed on to the *Scharnhorst* at a range of 27500 yards. The destroyers then received an order from the flagship at 16.38, to form up ready for a torpedo attack on the target on receipt of a signal from the *Duke of York*. The *Scharnhorst* was now 13 miles from the destroyers on a bearing of 020° and at 16.40 was 19300 yards from Force 1 on a bearing of 162°.

The *Belfast*, the only cruiser of Force 1 now in a position to join action, was ordered at 16.40 by Adm Fraser to prepare to illuminate the *Scharnhorst* with starshell. The *Belfast* complied, working up to her maximum speed.

Around the convoy, JW 55B, the U-boats were still in contact and reporting its position hourly. The HF/DF had fixed the position of a U-boat at 16.13 and again at 16.42, and the *Haida* and *Huron* were ordered to investigate the latter.

The trap for the *Scharnhorst* was now almost closed. She altered course to port and at 16.44 Force 2 shaped up on a course of 080° so that the firing arcs of all the turrets on the *Duke of York* were opened. The battlecruiser was now sandwiched between Forces 1 and 2 and at 16.47 the *Belfast* fired starshell to illuminate the target. This again failed to illuminate the battlecruiser due to the insufficient range of the shell, and so a minute later the *Duke of York* fired a starshell from one of her 5.25″ guns. This succeeded in illuminating the target, and as the battleship opened fire at a range of 12000 yards at 16.50, Adm Fraser sent off a sighting report.

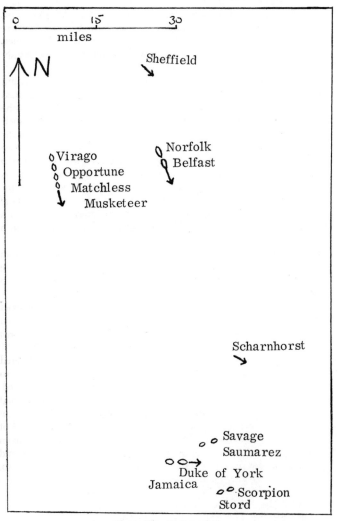

Fig. 9: The situation 16.50

The initial battleship action (16.50 to 17.27)

The illumination of the starshell fired from the port 5.25″ guns of the *Duke of York* was the first indication to the crew of the *Scharnhorst* that any heavy warships were near. Her radar aft had failed to detect Force 2 and she was caught unawares with her turrets trained fore and aft. On coming under fire from the battleship, the *Scharnhorst* altered course to the north at 16.55, and to conform Force 1 altered course to 180°, the 36th Division overtaking the *Norfolk* ½ mile to port, as they increased speed to 32 knots. Simultaneously the *Duke of York* swung round to 060° to comb the tracks of any torpedoes that might have been fired at her.

The *Jamaica* opened fire at 16.52 at a range of 13000 yards, straddling the battlecruiser with her third broadside, causing one hit. The first broadside from the *Duke of York* also straddled the *Scharnhorst*, one shell landing abreast A turret on the starboard bow and putting the turret out of action. The resulting fires flashed back into B turret and the powder handling room was partly flooded to prevent the flash setting off the cordite and blowing up the ship. A turret was now jammed in its firing position with the barrels elevated. A minute later another shell landed on the quarter deck, near to C turret, causing much superficial damage, destroying the aircraft and their hangar, and the shell splinters wiping out many of the AA guns' crews, whose survivors were then ordered by Capt Hintze to take cover. By this time the fires in A and B turrets had been extinguished and the powder room was drained.

Owing to the superior speed of the *Scharnhorst* the range gradually opened. As the Jamaica opened fire the *Scharnhorst* was sighted from the *Savage* who sent off a report and took up station to the south of the battlecruiser. The starshell from the *Duke of York* was now illuminating the *Savage* as well as the *Scharnhorst*, providing a good target for the battlecruiser to fire on, which she did, the shells falling 20 to 30 yards short of the destroyer.

At 16.57 Force 1 opened fire on the *Scharnhorst*, the *Belfast* firing one broadside and the *Norfolk* two. The *Belfast* then hauled round on to a course of 340° at 16.58, and prepared to fire torpedoes at the target. She was rejoined by the *Norfolk* at 17.00 but the *Sheffield* was still some way astern endeavouring to catch up and join the battle. In order to do so the *Sheffield* began to steer a more easterly course. At 1708 the *Scharnhorst* suddenly swung round on to an easterly course bearing 111° at a distance of 17000 yards. The *Belfast* and

HMS Duke of York firing her 14 in. guns.

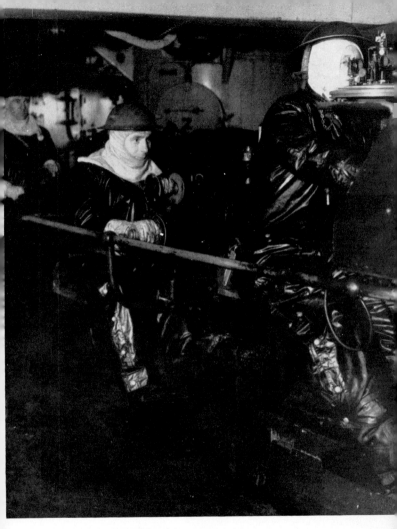

FACING PAGE: HMNoS Stord.
ABOVE: The crew of the torpedo tubes on
HMS Jamaica at action stations.

[J. S. White : Imperial War Museum

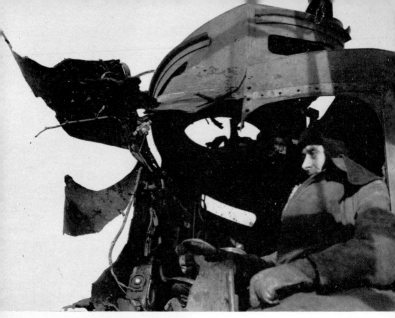

ABOVE: The director on HMS Saumarez *showing where the 11 in. shell from* Scharnhorst *passed through it.* LEFT: *Lt-Cdr E. N. Walmsley DSC, RN (right) CO of HMS* Saumarez *(he received a bar to his DSC after the action) with his First Lt —Lt J. E. Dyer, DSC, RN.*

[Imperial War Museum

ABOVE: The torpedo crew of HMS Jamaica. BELOW: The gun crews of HMS Duke of York.

[*Imperial War Museum*

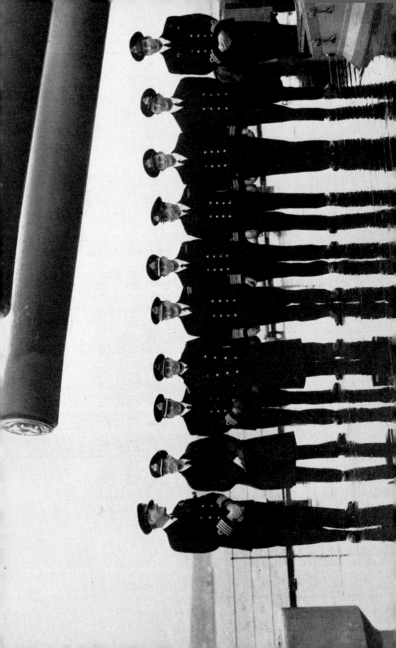

FACING PAGE: *Admiral Fraser with some of the COs of the ships: (l–r) Capt the Hon Guy Russell (Belfast), Cdr Lee Barber DSO (Opportune), Cdr E. L. Fisher DSO (Musketeer), Cdr Meyrick (Savage), Adm Sir Bruce Fraser (Duke of York), Capt. J. Hughes Hallett DSO (Jamaica), Lt–Cdr E. N. Walmsley DSC (Saumerez),* Lt–Cdr Clouston (Scorpion), Lt–Cdr White (Virago) *and* Lt Shaw (Matchless). ABOVE: *Survivors of Scharnhorst on HMS Duke of York.* BELOW: *A wounded survivor of Scharnhorst being transferred to a shore-bound ferry.*

Survivors of Scharnhorst *landing from the ferry.*   [*Imperial War Museum*

RIGHT: HMS Duke of York *leaving dock in 1943. BELOW: HMS* Belfast *in 1943.* [*Imperial War Museum : Real Photos*

TOP: *HMS* Sheffield. *ABOVE: HMS* Jamaica *in 1943. BELOW: HMS* Matchless.
[*Imperial War Museum : Real Photos : Imperial War Museum*

TOP: HMS Opportune. ABOVE:
HMS Savage (note twin 4.5 in. forward,
single 4.5 in. aft).   [Imperial War Museum

ABOVE: *HMS* Scorpion. *BELOW:*
HMS Virago.

Cammell Laird : Imperial War Museum

Scharnhorst in September 1939 after new bow has been fitted.

[Groner

ABOVE: Z30. BELOW: Z33 *in Norway.*
FACING PAGE: *Guns on the*
Scharnhorst.

[*Druppel* (2) : *Imperial War Museum*

ABOVE: *The radar array on HMS* Orwell. *In the lower foreground is the aerial array of a Type 285 gunnery radar set.* BELOW: *The picture presented on a gunnery radar screen. The target is shown by the inverted "V" on the right of the upper trace. The operator has matched the lower "V" and the range is thus transmitted automatically to the guns.*

[*Real Photos : Imperial War Museum*

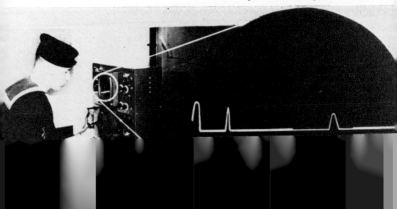

Norfolk conformed to this alteration of course of the target by steering a north and north-easterly course aimed at preventing her from heading back on a north-westerly course for the convoy. The battlecruiser replied to the fire of Force 1, firing two salvoes which landed near the cruisers' original course, before she ran out of range at 17.12. Force 1 ceased fire at this point, the *Belfast* having fired 5 salvoes from A and B turrets and two full broadsides using radar controlled fire.

By 17.10 the range between the *Scharnhorst* and the *Savage* had narrowed so much that the *Savage* sheered away to the south, no orders having yet been received to fire torpedoes. Three minutes later, however, Adm Fraser ordered the destroyers to close the target as soon as possible, and attack her with torpedoes. The target was now heavily obscured by smoke and after the tenth broadside when a delay occurred in illuminating the target due to the turrets firing starshell being changed, Adm Fraser resorted to blind fire. The *Scharnhorst* then changed to a mean course of 110° at 18.14, and two minutes later the *Savage* conformed by altering course to 090°. The destroyers found it impossible to attack the battlecruiser from the distance of 19000 yards, and they continued to chase the *Scharnhorst* from astern, working up to a maximum speed of 33 knots.

After engaging Force 1, the *Scharnhorst* concentrated on replying to the fire of Force 2, turning on to a southerly course to fire a broadside and then resuming her easterly course before firing the next broadside.

The two cruisers of Force 1 continued on their NNW course until 17.20 when they altered round to follow the *Scharnhorst* who was still on her easterly course. At the same time the *Musketeer* gave the destroyers of the 36th Division orders to attack the battlecruiser. On the *Scharnhorst* Rear-Adm Bey sent a signal to Adm Doenitz informing him that he was surrounded by heavy units. Just after this, at 17.26, Force 1 received orders from Adm Fraser to alter course to 140° and join Force 2. A minute later the cruisers altered round to their new south-easterly course, the *Sheffield* still being astern on a course of 130°, with the *Scharnhorst* on a bearing of 126° from her, steering a north-easterly course.

The chase (17.27 to 18.27)

Force 2 continued to chase the *Scharnhorst* to the east, firing broadsides at the battlecruiser, as her higher speed gradually opened the range. By 17.30 Force 2 was to the south-west of the target engaging and conforming to her movements, while the four "S" class destroyers were still trying to reach an attacking position. They were still, however, well astern of the *Scharnhorst*. The *Savage* and *Saumarez* were approaching from the port side and the other two destroyers were aiming to attack from the starboard side, all vessels taking avoiding action when fired on by the battlecruiser. To the NNW the 36th Division was gradually closing on a course parallel to the target, in an attempt to synchronise their attack with the destroyers of Force 2. Still farther away to the north-west Force 1 was steering a south-easterly course to join Force 2, with the *Sheffield* some distance behind.

By 17.42 the range had increased to 18000 yards and the *Jamaica* then ceased fire, having expended 19 broadsides at the target. During the action she had followed the *Duke of York*'s movements, keeping at a distance of 1050 yards on either her engaged or disengaged quarter. She avoided following directly in the battleship's wake in order to avoid the possibility of being hit by shells from the *Scharnhorst*, whose ranging on the battleship had now become much more accurate. In order to fire full broadsides, X and Y turrets of the *Duke of York* were being trained on their extreme forward bearing. (It was found after the action that the blast from these had found its way down the ventilation trunking and gutted the wardroom and destroyed the Admiral's private motor boat.) At 17.56 Adm Fraser ordered Vice-Adm Burnett to keep Force 1 to the north of the *Scharnhorst*, which he did, making the necessary alteration of course.

The salvoes from the *Duke of York* were being well directed. With A turret on the *Scharnhorst* out of action, B turret was the next to go. A 14" shell pierced the ventilation trunking to the turret, causing huge clouds of choking cordite fumes to fill the turret every time the guns were fired, soon making the turret inoperable. A second shell made a direct hit on the first of the starboard 5.9" guns, destroying the gun and sending jagged splinters into the magazine where all the crew were killed. Yet another shell entered No. 1 boiler room just above the waterline, severing a vital steam pipe to the turbines. With pressure reduced to practically nothing the speed of the huge battlecruiser fell right away to a mere 10 knots. The fractured pipe was soon isolated, however, by Cdr Otto Konig, the chief engineer, and the *Scharnhorst* increased speed to 22 knots. This last hit occurred at 18.20, when the range had opened to 20000 yards. The *Scharnhorst* ceased

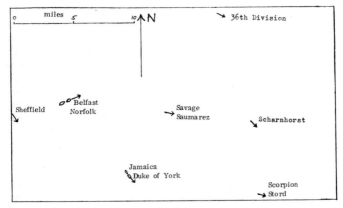

Fig. 10: The situation 18.24

fire at this point, just as Force 2 altered course to the south-east, towards Norway, to block the escape route of the *Scharnhorst*. The *Scharnhorst* was not the only vessel to be damaged during this part of the action. Two 11″ shells from one of her salvoes passed through the masts of the *Duke of York*, severing all the wireless aerials, and more serious still, the wires leading from the radar scanner to the Type 284 gunnery control radar set. Lt H. R. K. Bates RNVR climbed the mast and managed to repair the broken wires, restoring the radar sets' vision. Around this time the line of accuracy of the 14″ guns began to deteriorate when the yaw of 4° of the battleship began to cause a certain amount of trouble, and at 18.24 she ceased fire when the range was 21400 yards. By now she had fired 52 broadsides.

While the *Scharnhorst* was slowing down due to her ruptured steam pipes, the four destroyers of Force 2 closed to 12000 yards and began to catch up on the battlecruiser. Rear-Adm Bey now knew that he was cornered and at 18.24 he and Capt Hintze sent a last message to Adolf Hitler saying—"We shall fight to our last shell".

The first destroyer attack (18.27 to 18.50)
At 18.27 the *Savage* informed the *Saumarez*, who was 1500 yards on her starboard quarter, that the 1st Sub-Division of destroyers would attack the *Scharnhorst* with torpedoes from the west.

The *Scharnhorst* altered course to the south at 18.29 and Adm

Fraser, noting the reduction in speed of the battlecruiser at 18.38, immediately altered course to steer directly for the ship which was closed rapidly.

The four "S" class destroyers were still slowly closing up on the battlecruiser and at 18.40 were about 10000 yards from the target, the *Savage* and *Saumarez* (1st Sub-Division) being astern of the *Scharnhorst*, and the *Scorpion* and *Stord* (2nd Sub-Division) on her starboard side. The *Scharnhorst* observed the 1st Sub-Division closing and opened heavy fire on the two destroyers with her secondary armament of 5.9″, 4.1″, 40mm and 20mm. The fire, however, was poorly controlled, contradictory orders being given to the guns crews', owing to disagreements between the gunnery officers, the two destroyers suffering little damage.

The *Saumarez* returned the fire, when the range had closed to 7000 yards, claiming several hits from the 46 rounds fired from A, B and X guns. (Y gun was not bearing.)

Approaching from the north-west the *Savage* and *Saumarez* drew the battlecruiser's fire while the *Scorpion* and *Stord* slipped in unseen from the south-east. The *Scharnhorst* was now on a bearing of 100° from the *Savage* at a range of 5000 yards. The target was heavily obscured by smoke and the 1st Sub-Division was ordered to train its torpedo tubes to port at 18.51. As they emerged from the smoke the *Savage* fired starshell from X turret to illuminate the target, which was at once seen to have altered course to the south. This was in order to comb the tracks of the torpedoes that the 2nd Sub-Division had just fired. As the 2nd Sub-Division turned to starboard both destroyers fired full salvoes of eight torpedoes at 18.50, the *Scorpion* at a range of 2100 yards and the *Stord* at 1800 yards. The guns also opened fire, *Scorpion* firing three salvoes and the *Stord* a few more. Some hits were observed on the after superstructure of the *Scharnhorst*.

The *Scharnhorst*, having now sighted the 2nd Sub-Division, opened fire on the two destroyers, but failed to hit them, the destroyers returning the fire and scoring several hits on the superstructure of the battlecruiser.

The 1st Sub-Division meanwhile, seeing that the target had altered course to the south, immediately retrained their torpedo tubes to starboard, and at 18.55 turned to fire them. The *Scharnhorst* now realising that the attack of the 1st Sub-Division was the more dangerous of the two (the 1st Sub-Division had crept in much closer

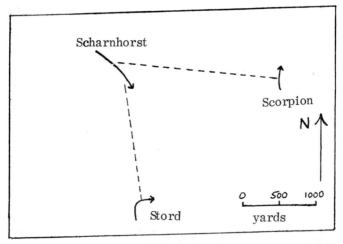

Fig. 11A: The situation 18.49

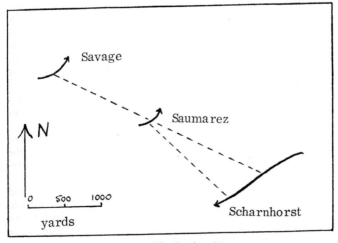

Fig. 11B: The situation 18.55

while the battlecruiser's attention was diverted to the 2nd Sub-Division) turned her entire armament on the two destroyers. The *Savage* fired a full salvo of torpedoes at a range of 3500 yards, but the *Saumarez* was only able to fire four torpedoes at a range of 1800 yards, at 18.56. Ranging on the *Saumarez*, the *Scharnhorst* scored several hits with her 11" shells, one passing through the director and another under the rangefinder, putting them both out of action. Fortunately the shells did not explode. More shells landed in the sea alongside the destroyer, splinters sweeping the decks of the vessel and decimating the torpedomen on the open deck. The hull was punctured in a number of places, but the holes were fortunately above the waterline. There was now only enough men left to man one set of torpedo tubes, the other tubes not being able to be trained owing to casualties in the crew and being of doubtful operating value as they were full of holes. Damage to the starboard engine of *Saumarez*, also caused by shell splinters, reduced the speed of the vessel to 10 knots on just the port engine. In all one officer and 10 ratings were killed and 11 ratings wounded.

The *Saumarez* then turned away making smoke to cover her withdrawal. In addition to this smoke, a smoke float aft on X gun deck was set off making it appear as though there was a fire aft. Thinking the destroyer was on fire it was decided to flood the after magazine and shell room.

As the *Savage* turned to withdraw, having fired her torpedoes, Y gun opened fire, one salvo being fired by director control, followed by eight more salvoes in local control. Just then three underwater explosions were heard in the *Duke of York*. One torpedo from the *Scorpion* hit the *Scharnhorst* just for'ard of the bridge on the starboard side and was closely followed by three torpedoes from the 1st Sub-Division exploding on the port side. These hits had a devastating effect on the battlecruiser. One exploded alongside a boiler room and damaged a shaft, reducing the speed of the vessel to 22 knots. Another torpedo hit the vessel aft flooding a number of compartments and a third torpedo struck her on the bows. These hits virtually sealed the fate of the *Scharnhorst*, as she was now incapable of steaming faster than the *Duke of York*.

Following the attack the destroyers withdrew to the north, while the *Scharnhorst* continued on her southerly course, her speed gradually decreasing.

Just as the destroyers completed their torpedo attack the *Norfolk* fired two broadsides at the battlecruiser, but then checked fire as so many echoes were showing on her radar screen.

The second battleship action (19.00)

Force 2 had steadily been closing up on the *Scharnhorst* while the destroyers were carrying out their torpedo attack. Now at 19.01, when the 284 radar set was reported back in action, the *Duke of York* and *Jamaica* opened fire at a range of 10400 yards. Almost at once hits were scored on the target, the first salvo straddling the battlecruiser and the second passing through the fantail and the remains of the aircraft hangar, setting off further fires and explosions. The *Scharnhorst* at once turned her remaining serviceable armament away from the destroyers to Force 2, when the range had closed to 8000 yards. The remaining 11″ ammunition from A and B turrets was moved aft to serve C turret, B turret having had to be abandoned due to the cordite fumes (see page 50).

At 19.07 Force 1 altered course to 180° to open the angle between Force 1, Force 2 and the *Scharnhorst*, so that Force 1 could open fire without danger to Force 2. The *Savage* rejoined the *Duke of York* at 19.10 forming up in line astern of the battleship.

By 19.11 the speed of the *Scharnhorst* had dropped to 10 knots and the vessel had developed a distinct list to starboard. About this time a last signal was received from Adm Doenitz, informing Rear-Adm Bey that submarines and destroyers were being ordered to the scene of the action at full speed.

At 19.12 Vice-Adm Burnett was ordered to assist in engaging the *Scharnhorst*, and three minutes later the *Belfast* opened fire on the battlecruiser at a range of 17000 yards, appearing to score two hits with her third broadside. Soon after, C turret on the *Scharnhorst* ceased firing, leaving just one or two 5.9″ guns to carry on the action.

The cruiser torpedo attack (19.17)

Force 1 altered course to the west at 19.17, when the *Belfast* had fired five 12 gun broadsides. Three minutes later they altered course to the south. A signal was then received from Adm Fraser ordering Vice-Adm Burnett to sink the *Scharnhorst* with torpedoes. *Belfast* then closed to 6200 yards on a course of 075° at 25 knots, and at 19.26 fired three torpedoes from the starboard tubes, on a bearing of 170°. At this point the target appeared to be almost stopped. Having fired the starboard tube the *Belfast* then hauled round to port to fire the port tubes.

Meanwhile the *Jamaica* had also been carrying out her torpedo attack. She altered course to comply with the order, and ceased fire from her main armament, having fired 22 broadsides, so as to approach the battlecruiser unseen. At 19.25 she turned to starboard and fired two of her port torpedo tubes, C tube having a misfire due to an improperly closed breech. The range was 3500 yards, but no hits were observed, as the speed of the *Scharnhorst* had been misjudged. The Type 272 radar now developed a fault due to gun blast, but as the cruiser turned to fire her starboard tubes, both 6″ and 4″ guns opened fire, getting off 36 rounds of 6″ at ranges between 3500 and 5000 yards. Many hits on the target were seen which replied with all her serviceable armament. Her shooting was wild, however, and the *Jamaica* suffered no damage.

As *Jamaica* reached the firing position for her starboard tubes the target could not be seen, and so the cruiser continued to turn until the *Scharnhorst* came into sight at 19.37, when *Jamaica* fired her three starboard tubes. The battlecruiser had by this time ceased firing.

Having fired her torpedoes *Jamaica* turned to join the *Duke of York*. At 19.35 the *Belfast* reached the required position to fire her port torpedo tubes but there was such a confusion of ships around the target, the 36th Division having arrived on the scene, that the *Belfast* hauled round to starboard, to the south, and began to approach the battlecruiser on a course of 160° preparing to fire her remaining torpedoes.

The 36th Division torpedo attack (19.33)

While the *Jamaica* and *Belfast* were making their torpedo attacks, the *Duke of York* ceased fire at 19.30, to allow the cruisers to close in on the target. The 36th Division had also reached the scene of the action by now, and at 19.33 *Musketeer* was only 1000 yards from the *Scharnhorst*. By 19.30 the speed of the battlecruiser was less than five knots, and her course wandered first to the north and then to the south. The starboard list had become so great that none of the guns could now be brought to bear, and so Capt Hintze ordered those of the crew still alive to abandon ship.

The 36th Division had been chasing the *Scharnhorst* all the afternoon. Cdr Fisher in the *Musketeer* had hoped to synchronise his torpedo attack with that of the "S" class destroyers, but was unable to make W/T contact with them. The 36th Division was thus still well astern when the *Savage* made her attack, but after the alteration of course made by the *Scharnhorst* and her reduction in speed the range closed rapidly, the two sub-divisions arriving in the target area just as the *Belfast* and *Jamaica* were completing their torpedo attack.

Closing from the north the two sub-divisions approached the *Scharnhorst* from astern, the 71st Sub-Division (*Musketeer* and *Matchless*) attacking the port side, and the 72nd Sub-Division (*Opportune* and *Virago*) the starboard. By now the target was only just moving along at three knots, with her starboard rail under water and the bows submerged.

Closing to a range of 1000 yards the *Musketeer* fired four torpedoes to starboard at 19.33, and saw three explosions on the target, between the funnel and the mainmast. Turning to withdraw, the *Matchless* was followed in by the *Musketeer*. She, however, was unable to fire any torpedoes, as a short time before a huge wave breaking over the waist of the vessel had damaged the training gear of the torpedo tubes. In addition to this heavy sea another had struck the bridge severing all communications with the torpedo tubes. As a result the order to train the tubes to starboard failed to reach the officer in charge in time, and so the *Matchless* hauled round to attack the target from the port bow.

The 72nd Sub-Division attacked simultaneously with the 71st, but from the starboard side. At a range of 2100 yards the *Opportune* fired four torpedoes at 19.31, to be followed at 19.33 by a further four torpedoes, fired at a range of 2500 yards. Claiming one hit from each of these salvoes the *Opportune* was followed by the *Virago*, who fired seven torpedoes at a range of 2800 yards at 19.34. Claiming two hits from her salvo, the *Opportune* and *Virago* then withdrew to the west, the *Virago* opening fire on the target, but checking after 10 rounds, when the *Scharnhorst* was observed to be lying stopped and not returning the fire.

The *Scharnhorst* sinks (19.45)
All that could be seen of the target now was a dull glow coupled with the sound of intermittent explosions. A thick pall of smoke hung around the battlecruiser, which not even the searchlights or starshell could penetrate. About 19.45 a tremendous explosion was heard and felt, as the magazine of the battlecruiser blew up, and as the *Belfast* arrived to make her second torpedo attack at 19.48, firing starshell as

she approached, the target had vanished. The *Matchless*, also arriving to deliver a torpedo attack, failed to locate the *Scharnhorst* too and she joined the *Scorpion* in rescuing survivors.

The *Jamaica* joined the *Duke of York* to the north of the target area, while the destroyers, *Belfast* and *Norfolk*, searched the area for survivors until 20.40. *Scorpion* rescued 30 of the crew and at one time was in sight of the Captain and Commander of the *Scharnhorst*. Capt Hintze was dead when reached and the Commander—Cdr Dominik—although able to grasp a life-line, had not the strength to hold on, and died before he could be hauled in.

Just after 21.00 the *Sheffield* rejoined Force 1, forming up astern of the *Norfolk* at 21.11. The whole Force then set course to 340° to resume covering JW 55B, increasing speed to 22 knots at 22.35 and altering course to 135°. The *Jamaica* after rejoining the *Duke of York* was ordered to join Force 1, but this order was rescinded and she proceeded independently for Kola.

During the morning of December 27th the south-westerly wind reached gale force, and just before daybreak aircraft echoes were detected on the radar plot of Force 1, at 08.50. At 09.14 the *Belfast* fired on an unidentified aircraft. A signal was then sent to SBNO North Russia requesting air cover.

The *Matchless* and *Musketeer* joined company with Force 1 at 12.30, and an hour later the ships arrived at Toros Island, proceeding up the harbour to anchor in Vaenga Bay.

The *Savage* and *Scorpion* joined up with the crippled *Saumarez* at 21.15 on December 26th. The *Saumarez* had gradually been increasing speed since the end of the action, and at 23.00 the three destroyers set a course of 090° at 15 knots, finally arriving at Kola at 20.00 on the 27th.

The convoy arrives intact, December 26th to 28th, 1943

During the evening of December 26th, while the *Duke of York* was engaging the *Scharnhorst*, the U-boats continued to remain in contact with JW 55B and report its position. The *Wrestler* was sent to search for one of these U-boats that was shadowing the convoy from ahead. This was the third submarine definitely detected during the day, and the *Wrestler* swept for the submarine to a depth of 2 miles on a bearing of 165°. At 23.15 the *Onslow* swept to a distance of 10 miles on a bearing of 155° in search of another U-boat and further transmissions were detected at 21.08 placing U-boats astern of the convoy.

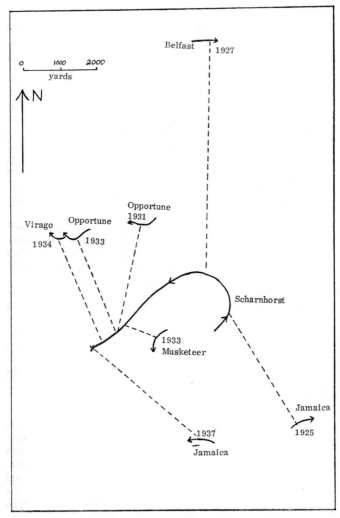

Fig. 12: The Scharnhorst *sinks*

The *Iroquois* was sent to search for a submarine at 21.27, sweeping to a depth of eight miles. The *Wrestler* was despatched yet again at 23.06 searching on a bearing of 285° to a depth of 10 miles, six miles on the beam of the convoy. These searches all proved fruitless, however.

Further fixes were obtained during the night and later the *Scourge* was sent to sweep for a contact detected at 04.54. Searching to a depth of six miles the *Scourge* found nothing and gradually the number of HF/DF contacts decreased as the U-boats obeyed orders to proceed to the area of the sinking of the *Scharnhorst*. By 10.00 it appeared that there was only one submarine shadowing the convoy, on the starboard quarter.

Daylight on December 27th showed that two ships had lost contact with the convoy when it altered course during the night. For the rest of that day JW 55B forged its way steadily through a south-westerly gale. At 06.15 the following morning, December 28th, the *Onslow* and *Wrestler* picked up a radar contact three miles on the starboard bow of the convoy. This turned out to be the *Ocean Valour*, one of the two ships that became detached during the night of the 26th. During the morning of the 28th the convoy was redisposed in three columns ready to enter the White Sea. Three destroyers, the *Haida*, *Huron* and *Iroquois*, were sent on ahead at 12.00, as they had very little fuel remaining in their tanks.

The local escort was detected at 16.30, joining the convoy at 17.50, the ships arriving safely the following morning at 10.30 to be followed by the straggler—*Ocean Gypsy*. Thus ended Operation FV.

HMS Savage

PART II
STATISTICAL DATA

Fig. 13: The sailing disposition of JW 55B

Merchant ship positions:

1. *Fort Nakasley*
2. *Ocean Valour*
3. *John J. Abel*
4. *Bernard N. Baker*
5. *Fort Vercheres*
6. *Cardinal Gibbons*
7. *John Wanamaker*
8. *Fort Kullyspell*
9. *Norlys*
10. *Brockholst Livingstone*
11. *John Vining*
12. *Thomas V. Walter*
13. *British Statesman*
14. *Ocean Messenger*
15. *Harold Winslow*
16. *Ocean Pride*
17. *Ocean Gypsy*
18. *Ocean Viceroy*
19. *Will Rogers*

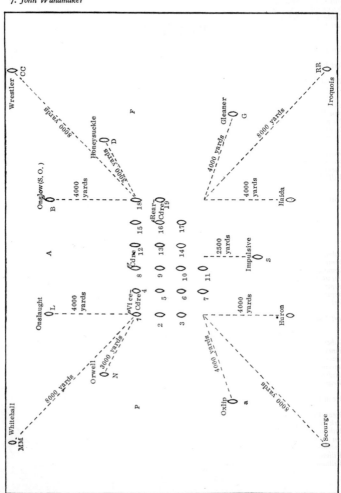

TABLE I. THE COMPOSITION OF THE CONVOYS

Convoy JW 55B:

Ship	Type	Flag	Owner	Tonnage gross/net	Built
Bernard N. Baker	SC	USA	USWA	7200/4384	1943
British Statesman	ST	UK	British Tanker Co	6991/4150	1923
Brockholst Livingstone	SC	USA	USWA	7176/4380	1942
Cardinal Gibbons	SC	USA	USWA	7191/4389	1942
Fort Kullyspell	SC	UK	MOWT (on bare boat charter) Owned Canadian Govt. Managed Hall Bros.	7190/4248	1943
Fort Nakasley	SC	UK	MOWT (on bare boat charter) Owned J. & J. Denholm	7100/4200	1943
Fort Vercheres	SC	UK	MOWT (on bare boat charter) Owned WSA. Managed Hain SS.	7122/4259	1942
Harold L. Winslow	SC	USA	USWA	7176/4380	1943
Norlys	MT	Panama	Tanker Corporation	9613/6051	1936
John J. Abel	SC	USA	USWA	7200/4384	1943
John Vining	SC	USA	USWA	7191/4360	1942
John Wanamaker	SC	USA	USWA	7176/4380	1943
Ocean Gypsy	SC	UK	MOWT. J. & C. Harrison	7178/4280	1942
Ocean Messenger	SC	UK	MOWT. Watts Watts & Co Ltd	7178/4280	1942
Ocean Pride	SC	UK	MOWT. Sir W. R. Smith & Sons Ltd	7173/4278	1942
Ocean Valour	SC	UK	MOWT. W. A. Souter & Co Ltd	7174/4272	1942
Ocean Viceroy	SC	UK	MOWT. P. Henderson & Co	7174/4272	1942
Thomas U. Walter	SC	USA	USWA	7176/4380	1943
Will Rogers	SC	USA	USWA	7200/4384	1942

Convoy RA 55A:

Ship	Type	Flag	Owner	Tonnage gross/net	Built
Arthur L. Perry	SC	USA	USWA	7176/4380	1943
Daniel Drake	SC	USA	USWA	7176/4380	1943
Edmund Fanning	SC	USA	USWA	7176/4380	1943
Empire Carpenter	SC	UK	MOWT. Hain SS	7025/4857	1943
Empire Celia	SC	UK	MOWT. Connell & Grace Ltd	7025/4856	1943
Empire Nigel	SC	UK	MOWT	7067/4867	1943
Fort McMurray	SC	UK	MOWT (on bare boat charter) Owned Morel Ltd	7133/4244	1942
Fort Yukon	SC	UK	MOWT (on bare boat charter) Owned Canadian Govt. Managed Capper, Alexander & Co	7153/4240	1943
Gilbert Stuart	SC	USA	USWA	7176/4374	1943
Henry Villard	SC	USA	USWA	7176/4374	1942
James Smith	SC	USA	USWA	7181/4384	1942
Junecrest	SC	UK	Crest Shipping Co Ltd	6945/4159	1942
Mijdrecht	MT	Dutch	N. V. Maats	7493/4398	1931
Ocean Strength	SC	UK	MOWT. Managed J. & J. Denholm Ltd	7173/4278	1942
Ocean Vanity	SC	UK	MOWT. Managed Raeburn & Varel Ltd	7174/4272	1942
Ocean Verity	SC	UK	MOWT. Managed A. Holt & Co	7174/4272	1942
Park Holland	SC	USA	USWA	7176/4380	1943
Rathlin	SC	UK	Clyde Shipping Co Ltd	1600/697	1936
San Adolfo	MT	UK	Eagle Oil & Shipping Co Ltd	7365/4376	1935
Thomas Sim Lee	SC	USA	USWA	7191/4389	1942
William L. Marcy	SC	USA	USWA	7176/4380	1942
William Windom	SC	USA	USWA	7191/4380	1943

Table 2. BRITISH FORCES
Escorts for Convoy JW 55B:

Type	Ship	Commanding Officer	Squadron
Local Escort			
Corvette	HMS *Borage*		Western Approaches Command
,,	HMS *Wallflower*		
Minesweeper	HMS *Hound* (SO		18 M/S Flotilla
,,	HMS *Hydra*		,,
Through Escort			
Destroyer	HMS *Whitehall*	Lt-Cdr P. J. Cowell DSC	Western Approaches Command
,,	HMS *Wrestler*	Lt R. W. B. Lacon DSC	,,
Corvette	HMS *Honeysuckle*	Lt H. H. D. MacKilligan DSC RNR	,,
,,	HMS *Oxlip*	Lt-Cdr C. W. Leadbetter RNR	,,
Minesweeper	HMS *Gleaner* (SO)	Lt-Cdr F. J. S. Hewitt DSC	,,
Fighting Destroyer Escort			
Destroyer	HMCS *Haida*	Cdr H. G. de Wolf RCN	
,,	HMCS *Huron*	Lt-Cdr H. S. Rayner DSC RCN	
,,	HMS *Impulsive*	Lt-Cdr P. Bekenn	
,,	HMCS *Iroquois*	Cdr J. C. Hibberd DSC RCN	
,,	HMS *Onslaught*	Cdr W. H. Selby DSC	
,,	HMS *Onslow* (SO)	Capt J. A. McCoy DSO (Capt D 17)	
,,	HMS *Orwell*	Lt-Cdr J. A. Hodges DSO	
,,	HMS *Scourge*	Lt-Cdr G. L. M. Balfour	

Escorts for Convoy RA 55A:

Type	Ship	Commanding Officer	Squadron
Local Escort			
Through Escort			
Destroyer	HMS *Beagle*	Lt-Cdr N. R. Murch	Western Approaches Command
,,	HMS *Westcott*	Cdr H. Lambton RN (RTD)	,,
Corvette	HMNoS *Andenes*		,,
,,	HMS *Dianella*	Temporary Lt J. F. Tognola RNR	,,
,,	HMS *Poppy*	Temporary Lt D. R. C. Onslow RNR	,,
Minesweeper	HMS *Seagull*	Lt-Cdr R. W. Ellis DSC	,,
Fighting Destroyer Escort			
Destroyer	HMS *Ashanti*	Lt-Cdr J. R. Barnes	
,,	HMCS *Athabaskan*	Lt-Cdr J. H. Stubbs DSO RCN	
,,	HMS *Matchless*	Lt W. S. Shaw	36 Destroyer Division
,,	HMS *Meteor*	Lt-Cdr D. J. P. Jewitt	,,
,,	HMS *Milne* (SO)	Capt I. M. R. Campbell DSO (Capt D)	,,
,,	HMS *Musketeer*	Cdr R. L. Fisher DSO OBE	36 Destroyer Division
,,	HMS *Opportune*	Cdr J. Lee-Barber DSO	,,
,,	HMS *Virago*	Lt-Cdr A. J. R. White	,,

Scouting Force for Convoys JW 55B and RA 55A:

Type	Ship	Commanding Officer	Squadron
Force 1			
Cruiser	HMS *Belfast* (SO)	Vice-Adm R. L. Burnett CB, DSO, OBE	10 Cruiser Squadron
		Capt F. R. Parham	
,,	HMS *Norfolk*	Capt D. K. Bain	,,
,,	HMS *Sheffield*	Capt C. T. Addis	,,

Distant Cover for Convoys JW 55B and RA 55A

Type	Ship	Commanding Officer	Squadron
Force 2			
Battleship	HMS *Duke of York* (Flagship)	C-in-C Home Fleet Adm Sir Bruce Fraser KCB, KBE	Flagship Home Fleet
		Capt the Hon G. H. E. Russell CBE	
Cruiser	HMS *Jamaica*	Capt J. Hughes-Hallett DSO	
Destroyer	HMS *Saumarez*	Lt-Cdr E. W. Walmsley DSC	
,,	HMS *Savage*	Cdr M. D. G. Meyrick	
,,	HMS *Scorpion*	Lt-Cdr W. S. Clouston	
,,	HMNOS *Stord*	Lt-Cdr S. Storeheill RNO	

TABLE 2A. SHIPS' DATA

DUKE OF YORK

Displacement	38000 tons standard, 44460 tons full load.
Dimensions	700 (pp) (wl) 745 (oa) × 103 × 35½ feet.
Machinery	8 Admiralty three drum boilers (lb/in.² at); 4 shafts; single reduction geared turbines, 125000 SHP=29¼ knots.
	3842 tons oil, radius 6300 miles at 20 knots or 3200 miles at 27 knots.
Protection	Main belt 5½ in. (fwd)/15 in. (mag)/14 in. (mach)/4½ in. (aft), deck 6 in. (over mag)/5 in. (over mach), turrets 15 in. (side)/16 in. (face)/9 in. (roof), barbettes 16 in., 5·25 in. turrets 6 in., CT 16 in.
Armament	10–14 in./45 cal (2×4+1×2), 16–5·25 in./50 cal (8×2), 8–40mm (2×4), 16–20mm (8×2), 88–2 pdr (8×8+6×4) guns; 4 Supermarine Walrus seaplanes and 1 catapult.
Complement	1640.

Name	Builder	Laid Down	Launched	Completed	Fate
Duke of York (ex-*Anson*)	J. Brown	5.5.37	28.2.40	11.41	Scrapped Faslane 1958

NORFOLK

Displacement	9925 tons standard.
Dimensions	590 (pp) (wl) 630 (oa) × 66 × 17 feet.
Machinery	8 Admiralty three drum boilers (lb/in.² at); 4 shafts; geared Parsons turbines, 80000 SHP=32¼ knots.
	3200 tons oil, radius.

Protection	Deck 4 in., turrets 2 in. (face)/$1\frac{1}{2}$ in. (side), CT 3 in.
Armament	8–8 in./50 cal (4×2), 8–4 in./45 cal (4×2), 2–40mm (1×2), 8–20mm (8×1), 16–2 pdr (2×8) guns; 8–21 in. TT (2×4); 1 Supermarine Walrus seaplane and 1 catapult.
Complement	650.

Name	Builder	Laid Down	Launched	Completed	Fate
Norfolk	Fairfield	7.27	12.12.28	6.30	Scrapped Newport 1950

BELFAST

Displacement	11550 tons standard.
Dimensions	579 (pp) (wl) $613\frac{1}{2}$ (oa)×66×17 feet.
Machinery	4 Admiralty three drum boilers (lb/in.² at); 4 shafts; geared Parsons turbines, 80000 SHP= 32 knots. 2260 tons oil, radius 8000 miles at 14 knots.
Protection	Main belt 3 to 5 in., deck 2 in., turrets $2\frac{1}{2}$ in. (face)/1 in. (side), CT 4 in.
Armament	12–6 in./50 cal (4×3), 12–4 in./45 cal (6×2), –40mm ( ), –20mm ( ), 16–2 pdr (2×8) guns; 6–21 in. TT (2×3); 3 Supermarine Walrus seaplanes and 1 catapult.
Complement	850.

Name	Builder	Laid Down	Launched	Completed	Fate
Belfast	Harland & Wolff	10.12.36	17.3.38	3.8.39	In reserve 1969. Future undecided

SHEFFIELD

Displacement	9100 tons standard, 12400 tons full load.
Dimensions	558 (pp) 584 (wl) $591\frac{1}{2}$ (oa)×64×17 feet.
Machinery	4 Admiralty three drum boilers (lb/in.² at); 4 shafts; geared Parsons turbines, 75000 SHP= $32\frac{1}{4}$ knots. 1970 tons oil, radius 7000 miles at 14 knots.
Protection	Main belt 3 to 4 in., deck 2 in., turrets 2 in. (face)/1 in. (side), CT 4 in.
Armament	12–6 in./50 cal (4×3), 8–4 in./45 cal (4×2), 20–40mm (6×2+8×1), –20mm (×1), 8–2 pdr (2×4) guns; 6–21 in. TT (2×3); 3 Supermarine Walrus seaplanes and 1 catapult.
Complement	700.

Name	Builder	Laid Down	Launched	Completed	Fate
Sheffield	Vickers-Armstrong	31.1.35	23.7.36	25.8.37	Scrapped

JAMAICA

Displacement 8000 tons standard, 11270 tons full load.
Dimensions 538 (pp) 549 (wl) 555½ (oa) × 62 × 16½ feet.
Machinery 4 Admiralty three drum boilers (lb/in.² at   ); 4 shafts;
geared Parsons turbines, 72500 SHP = 31½ knots.
1620 tons oil, radius 6000 miles at 13 knots.
Protection Main belt 3 to 4½ in., deck 2 in., turrets 2 in., CT 4 in.
Armament 12–6 in./50 cal (4×3), 8–4 in./45 cal (4×2), 4–20mm (1×2+2×1),
8–2 pdr (2×4) guns; 6–21 in. TT (2×3); 3 Supermarine Walrus
seaplanes and 1 catapult.
Complement 730.

Name	Builder	Laid Down	Launched	Completed	Fate
Jamaica	Vickers-Armstrong	28.4.39	16.11.40	29.6.42	Scrapped 1960–1962

MATCHLESS and MUSKETEER

Displacement 1920 tons standard, 2441 tons full load.
Dimensions 345½ (pp) 354 (wl) 362½ (oa) × 36¾ × 13½ feet.
Machinery 2 Admiralty three drum boilers (300 lb/in.² at 660° F); 2 shafts;
single reduction Parsons turbines, 48000 SHP = 36½ knots.
567 tons oil, radius 5500 miles at 15 knots or 2250 miles at 25 knots.
Armament 6–4·7 in./   cal (3×2) (1550 shells), 10–20mm (4×2+2×1),
4–2 pdr (1×4) (7200 shells) guns; 8–21 in. TT (2×4); 42 depth
charges with 2 chutes and 2 throwers.
Complement 221.

Name	Builder	Laid Down	Launched	Completed	Fate
Matchless	A. Stephen	14.9.40	4.9.41	26.2.42	To Turkey 1958
Musketeer	Fairfield	7.12.39	2.12.41	18.9.42	Scrapped Sunderland 1955

OPPORTUNE

Displacement 1540 tons standard, 2220 tons full load.
Dimensions 328¾ (pp) 337 (wl) 345 (oa) × 35 × 12½ feet.
Machinery 2 Admiralty three drum boilers (300 lb/in.² at 630° F); 2 shafts;
single reduction Parsons turbines, 40000 SHP = 32 knots.
484 tons oil, 3850 miles at 20 knots.
Armament 4–4 in./   cal (4×1), 8–20mm (8×1), 4–2 pdr (1×4) guns; 8–21 in.
TT (2×4); 2 depth charge chutes and 2 throwers.
Complement 175.

Name	Builder	Laid Down	Launched	Completed	Fate
Opportune	Thornycroft	28.3.40	21.1.42	14.8.42	Scrapped Milford Haven 1955

SAVAGE

Displacement	1710 tons standard, 2530 tons full load.
Dimensions	339½ (pp) 348 (wl) 362¾ (oa) × 35¾ × 13 feet.
Machinery	2 Admiralty three drum boilers (300 lb/in.^{2} at 630° F); 2 shafts; single reduction Parsons turbines, 40000 SHP= 32 knots.
	484 tons oil, radius 5500 miles at 15 knots or 3700 miles at 20 knots.
Armament	4–4·5 in./ cal (1×2+2×1), 12–20mm (6×2) guns; 8–21 in. TT (2×4);
Complement	180.

Name	Builder	Laid Down	Launched	Completed	Fate
Savage	Hawthorne Leslie	7.12.41	24.9.42	8.6.43	Scrapped Newport 1962

SCORPION, SAUMAREZ, STORD

Displacement	As *Savage.*
Dimensions	As *Savage.*
Machinery	As *Savage.*
Armament	4–4·7 in./ cal (4×1), 40mm—*Saumarez*= 2
	Scorpion = 4
	Stord = 2
	20mm—*Saumarez*= 4 (4×1)
	Scorpion = 8 (8×1)
	Stord = 8 (8×1) guns;
	8–21 in. TT (2×4); 70 depth charges with 2 chutes and 4 throwers.
Complement	180 (*Saumarez* 225).

Name	Builder	Laid Down	Launched	Completed	Fate
Saumarez	Hawthorne Leslie	8.9.41	20.11.42	1.7.43	Scrapped Charlestown 1950
Scorpion (ex-*Sentinel*)	Cammell Laird	19.6.41	26.8.42	11.5.43	To Holland 1945
Stord (ex-*Success*)	J. S. White	25.2.42	3.3.43	6.9.43	To Norway on completion. Scrapped 1959

VIRAGO

Displacement	1710 tons standard, 2530 tons full load.
Dimensions	339½ (pp) 348 (wl) 362¾ (oa) × 35¾ × 13 feet.
Machinery	2 Admiralty three drum boilers (300 lb/in.^{2} at 630° F); 2 shafts; single reduction Parsons turbines, 40000 SHP= 32 knots.
	484 tons oil, radius 5500 miles at 15 knots or 3700 miles at 20 knots.
Armament	4–4·7 in./ cal (4×1), 2–40mm (1×2), 8–20mm (4×2) guns; 8–21 in. TT (2×4); 70 depth charges with 2 chutes and 4 throwers.
Complement	180.

Name	Builder	Laid Down	Launched	Completed	Fate
Virago	Swan Hunter	16.2.42	4.2.43	5.11.43	Converted to A/S frigate. S.E.

TABLE 3. GERMAN FORCES

Type	Ship	Commanding Officer	Squadron
Battle Group 1			
Battlecruiser	*Scharnhorst* (Flagship	C-in-C Rear Adm Erich A. Bey Capt Julius Hintze	
Destroyer	*Z29* (SO)	Capt Johannesson Lt-Cdr Mutius	4 Destroyer Flotilla
,,	*Z30*	Lt-Cdr Lampe	,,
,,	*Z33*	Capt Holtorf	,,
,,	*Z34*	Lt-Cdr Hetz	,,
,,	*Z38*	Lt-Cdr Brutzer	,,
Coastal Escort for Battle Group			
Motor-minesweeper	*R56*	Lt W. Maclot	5 Minesweeper Flotilla
,,	*R58*	Sub-Lt W. Hauss	,,
,,	*R121*		,,
U-boat Patrol			
Submarine	*U-277*	Lt Lubsen	Group "Eisenbart"
,,	*U-314*	Lt-Cdr Basse	,,
,,	*U-354*	Lt-Cdr Herbschleb	,,
,,	*U-387*	Lt-Cdr Buchler	,,
,,	*U-601*	Lt Hansen	,,
,,	*U-716*	Lt Dunkelberg	,,
,,	*U-957*		,,

TABLE 3A. SHIPS' DATA

SCHARNHORST

Displacement   31800 tons standard, 38900 tons full load.

Dimensions   741½ (wl) 771 (oa) × 98½ × 32½ feet.

Machinery   12 Wagner boilers (8 at 661 lb and 4 at 735 lb at 868° F); 3 shafts; geared Brown-Boveri turbines, 160000 SHP = 31½ knots. 6300 tons oil, radius 10000 miles at 17 knots or 8800 miles at 19 knots.

Protection   Krupp armour. Main belt 5 in. (fwd)/13 in. (amid)/3 in. (aft), upper deck 2 in., main deck 3¼ in. (slope)/4¼ in. (flat), 11 in., turrets 4 in. (rear)/9¾ in. (side)/14¼ in. (face), barbettes 14 in., 5·9 in. turrets 6 in., CT 14 in.

Armament   9–11 in./45 cal (3 × 3) (945 shells), 12–5·9 in./55 cal (4 × 2 + 4 × 1) (1800 shells), 14–4·1 in./65 cal (7 × 2) (5600 shells), 18–37mm (8 × 2) (32000 shells), 44–20mm AA (6 × 4 + 4 × 2 + 12 × 1) (76000 shells) guns; 6–21 in. TT (2 × 3); 4 Arado 196 seaplanes and 1 catapult.

Complement   1800.

Name	Builder	Laid Down	Launched	Completed	Fate
Scharnhorst	Wilhelmshaven Naval D.Y.	1934	3.10.36	7.1.39	Sunk British forces 26/12/43 North Cape 72° 16′ N– 28° 41′ E

Z29 and Z30

Displacement 2603 tons standard, 3597 tons full load.
Dimensions 393½ (pp) 400¼ (wl) 416¾ (oa) × 39¼ × 15 feet.
Machinery 6 Wagner boilers (1028 lb at 868° F); 2 shafts; geared Wagner turbines, 70000 = 38½ knots.
825 tons oil, radius 5900 miles at 19 knots.
Armament 5–5·9 in./48 cal (1 × 2 + 3 × 1) (600 shells), 6–37mm AA (2 × 2 + 2 × 1) (8000 shells), 8–20mm AA (2 × 4) (10000 to 12000 shells) guns; 8–21 in. TT (2 × 4); 60 mines.
Complement 321.

Name	Builder	Laid Down	Launched	Completed	Fate
Z29	AG Weser (Bremen)		15.10.40	25.6.41	Handed over to USN 1945. Scuttled off Skagerak 16.12.46
Z30	,,		8.12.40	15.11.41	Handed over to RN 1945 and used as experimental vessel until 1948

Z33, Z34, and Z38

Displacement 2603 tons standard, 3597 tons full load.
Dimensions 400¼ (wl) 416¾ (oa) × 39¼ × 15 feet.
Machinery 6 Wagner boilers (1028 lb at 868° F); 2 shafts; geared Wagner turbines, 70000 SHP = 38½ knots.
825 tons oil, radius 5900 miles at 19 knots.
Armament 5–5·9 in./48 cal (1 × 2 + 3 × 1) (600 shells), 6–37mm AA (2 × 2 + 2 × 1) (8000 shells), 8–20mm AA (2 × 4) (10000 to 12000 shells) guns; 8–21 in. TT (2 × 4); 60 mines.
Complement 320 (*Z38* 321).

Name	Builder	Laid Down	Launched	Completed	Fate
Z33	AG Weser (Bremen)		15.9.42	6.2.43	Handed over to USSR 1946. Renamed *Provorny*
Z34	,,		5.5.42	5.6.43	Handed over to USN 1945. Scuttled in North Sea 26.3.46
Z38	Germania Werft (Kiel)		5.8.41	20.3.43	Handed over to RN 1945. Renamed *Nonsuch*. Scrapped 1949

U–277, 314, 354, 387, 601, 716, 957. (TYPE VIIC)

Displacement 769/871 tons.
Dimensions 220¼ × 20¼ × 15¾ feet.
Machinery 2-shaft/diesel electric motors, BHP/SHP 2800/750 = 17/7½ knots.
114 tons oil, radius 6500/80 miles at 12/4 knots.

Armament   1–3·5 in., 1–37mm, 2–20mm (2×1) guns; 5–21 in. TT (4 bow, 1 stern with 14 torpedoes or 14 mines).

Complement   44.

Number	Builder	Laid Down	Launched	Completed	Fate
U-277	Bremer Vulkan		7.11.42	21.12.42	Lost 1.5.44
U-314	Flenderwerft		17.4.43	10.6.43	Lost 30.1.44
U-354	Flensburger		6.1.42	22.2.42	Lost 25.8.44
U-387	Howaldts Werke		1.10.42	24.11.42	Lost 9.12.44
U-601	Blohm & Voss		29.10.41	18.12.41	Lost 25.2.44
U-716	Stulcken Sohn		15.1.43	15.4.43	Surrendered and scuttled
U-957	Blohm & Voss		21.11.42	7.1.43	Lost accident 19.10.44

R56, R58, R121

Displacement   125 tons.

Dimensions   124 (oa) × 19 × 4½ feet.

Machinery   2 MAN diesels; 2 shafts; 1800 BHP = 21 knots.
10 tons oil, radius 1100 miles at 15 knots.

Armament   1–37mm (1000) shells, –20mm.

Complement   35.

Number	Builder	Laid Down	Launched	Completed	Fate
R56	Abeking & Rasmussen (Lemwerder)		28.9.40		Sunk by British MGB's off Bommelenfiord 8.12.44
R58	,,		25.10.40		To Russia 1946
R121	,,		11.3.43		To Russia 1946

TABLE 4. CHAIN OF COMMAND OF KRIEGSMARINE 1943

NAVAL STAFF
(BERLIN)

NAVAL GROUP NORTH
(KIEL)

FLAG OFFICER
NORTHERN WATERS
(NARVIK)

NAVAL COMMAND NORWAY
(OSLO)
(Not connected with direction of Fleet units. In command of coastal defence, M/L and M/S duties)

FLAG OFFICER
BATTLE GROUP

FLAG OFFICER
POLAR COAST

FLAG OFFICER
NORTH COAST

FLAG OFFICER
WEST COAST

TABLE 5
GUNS

Size (in.)	Length (cal)	Elevation	Rate of fire (rounds/min)	Weight of shell (lbs)	Muzzle velocity (feet/sec)	Range (yards)
British						
14	45	+45 −	2	1595	2400	36000
8	50	+70 −3	6	256	3000	29200
6	50	+35 −10		100	3000	
5·25	50	+75 −10	18	82	2600	22500
4·7		+50	10	62		
4·7		+55	10	50		
4·5		+80 − (twin mt) +55 − (single mt)		55		
4		+80		50		
4	45			31		
40mm	43	+90 −10	120	2	2300	2500
20mm						1000
2 pdr	40	+85 −5	200	2	2000	6600
German						
11	45	+45 −8	2 to 4	694	2953	46590
5·9	55	+35 −		100	2871	12670
5·9	48	+47 −19		88	2871	18590
4·1	65	+70 −8	20	$33\frac{1}{3}$	2953	11260
37mm	83		50		3280	7382
20mm					2952	2406

TABLE 6
GUNNERY

Ship	Calibre	Turret	Gun	Shells fired	B/S missed (inclusive)	Time	B/S numbers	Remarks
Duke of York	14″	A	1	5	5	16.49	1 to 6	Misfire
			2	5	6 to 8			Turret fault
			3	2	3 to 73			Shell cage fault and bad gun drill
			4	6	—			
		B	1	6				
			2	6				
		Y	1	6				
			2	6				
			3	6				
			4	5	2			
		A	1	9	10	17.00	7 to 16	Misfire Gun crew error
			2	5	14 to 19			Shell cage not ready
			3	0				
			4	10				
		B	1	10				
			2	10				
		Y	1	3			7 to 9	
			2	3				
			3	3				
			4	3				

Ship	Calibre	Turret	Gun	Shells fired	B/S missed (inclusive)	Time	B/S numbers	Remarks
		A	1	3		17.24	17 to 19	
			2	0				
			3	0				
			4	1	17 to 18			Misfire
		B	1	3				
			2	3				
		A	1	5		17.29	20 to 24	
			2	5				
			3	0				
			4	5				
		B	1	5				
			2	5				
		A	1	5		17.37	25 to 29	
			2	3	28 to 33			Shell cage not ready
			3	0				
			4	5				
		B	1	5				
			2	5				
		A	1	8		17.44	30 to 37	
			2	2	36 to 41			Shell cage not ready
			3	0				
			4	8				
		B	1	8				
			2	2	32 to 53			Rammer jammed
		Y	1	8				
			2	8				
			3	6	36 to 54			Recoil fault
			4	8				
		A	1	7		17.57	38 to 44	
			2	2	44 to 49			Shell cage not ready
			3	0				
			4	7				
		B	1	7				
			2	0				
		Y	1	7				
			2	7				
			3	0				
			4	7				
		A	1	5		18.10	45 to 49	
			2	0				
			3	0				
			4	4	49 to 51			Breech damaged, closed by hand
		B	1	5				
			2	0				
		Y	1	5				
			2	5				
			3	0				
			4	5				
		A	1	3		18.20	50 to 52	
			2	3				
			3	0				
			4	1				
		B	1	3				
			2	0				

Ship	Calibre	Turret	Gun	Shells fired	B/S missed (inclusive)	Time	B/S numbers	Remarks
		Y	1	3				
			2					
			3	0				
			4					
		A	1	3		19.00	53 to 62	7 B/S missed
			2	9				1 B/S missed
			3	0				
			4	7				3 B/S missed
		B	1	7				3 B/S missed
			2	1				8 B/S missed
		Y	1					
			2					
			3	3				7 B/S missed
			4	3				1 B/S missed
		A	1	18		19.12	63 to 80	
			2	13	65 to 69			Shell cage not ready
			3	4				
			4	10	63 to 65 68 to 70 & 76 to 77			Breech damaged, closed by hand
		B	1	18				
			2	18				
		Y	1	1	63 to 79			Ammunition hoist fault
			2	18				
			3	1	63 to 79			As Y 1
			4	1	63 to 79			As Y 1

Turret and gun number	Shells fired	Broadsides missed
A1	71	9
A2	47	33
A3	6	71
A4	64	16
B1	77	3
B2	50	30
Y1	33	17
Y2	47	
Y3	19	43
Y4	32	19
TOTAL	446	241

Overall number of broadsides fired during action = 80.

Time	Broadsides fired	Straddle	Over	Under	Rate of Fire BS/min	Remarks
16.49	6	4	1	2	½	Believed 1 hit
17.00	10	4	2	4	½	Blind firing from 10th B/S. 3 straddles resulted
17.24	3	3	0	0	¾	
17.29	5	3	1	1	⅝	
17.37	5	2 (& over) 1 (& under)	1	1	⅝	
17.44	8	3 1 (& under) 1 (& over)	1	1	½	Yaw of 4° caused difficulties and accuracy deteriorated
17.57	7	2	2	3	½	Range spotting difficult
18.10	5	1	3	1	½	
18.20	3	?	?	1		2 shots unobserved. Cease fire. 284 radar damaged by gun blast
19.00						14″ resumed firing—no log kept
19.12	18	11 1 (& short)	4	2		
19.30						Fire checked

Ship	Calibre	Turret	Gun	Shells fired	Time	B/S fired	Remarks
Duke of York	5·25″	Port 1	1	93	16·52 to 18·00	59	All SAP
			2	94			All SAP
		Port 2	1	69			58 SAP remainder starshell. Total of 40 rounds of starshell in port 2
			2	51	19·02 to 19·17	42	40 SAP remainder starshell
		Port 3	1	37			All starshell. Total of 60 rounds of starshell in port 3
			2	33			All starshell
		Port 4	1	84			All SAP
			2	74			All SAP
		Stbd 1	1	36	16·52 to 19·17	38	All SAP
			2	37			All SAP
		Stbd 2	1	17			7 SAP remainder starshell. Total of 40 rounds of starshell in stbd 2
			2	15			10 SAP remainder starshell
		Stbd 3	1	23			All starshell. Total of 60 rounds of starshell in stbd. 3
			2	23			All starshell
		Stbd 4	1	0			Not bearing
			2	0			Not bearing
		TOTAL		686			531 SAP 155 starshell

Ship	Calibre	Turret	Shells fired	Time	B/S fired	Shells fired	Remarks
Jamaica	6″	A	124	16.52 to 17.42	19	196	Fourteen of 4 turrets and five of 2 turrets
		B	126	19.04 to 19.19	22	229	Seventeen of 4 turrets and five of 2 turrets
		X	103	19.23 to 19.37	4	36	Two of 4 turrets and two of 2 turrets
		Y	108				
	4″		6				

TOTAL 6″ = 461
4″ = 6

Ship	Calibre	Turret	Shells fired	Time	B/S fired	Remarks
Sheffield	6″	A1	16	12.24 to 12.40	26	
		2	3			Breech jammed after third round and not cleared until after 12.40
		3	17			
		B1	14			
		B2	14			
		B3	15			
		X1	3			
		X2	3			
		X3	4			
		Y1	2			
		Y2	3			
		Y3	3			

TOTAL 97

Ship	Calibre	Shells fired	B/S fired
Belfast	6″	316	38
	4″	77	
Norfolk	8″	161	31

Total ammunition expenditure:
14″ = 446
5·25″ = 531 SAP + 155 starshell
8″ = 161
6″ = 974
4″ = 83

Ship	Calibre	Turret	Shells fired	Salvoes fired
Saumarez	4·7″	A	14	
		B	22	
		X	12	
		Y	0	
Savage	4·5″	Y	16	8
Scorpion	4·7″			3
Stord	4·7″		No. unknown	
Virago	4·7″	A, B+X	10	6 (in addition to the 10 rounds)
Musketeer	4·7″		52	

NOTES TO BRITISH GUNNERY

On board the flagship—HMS *Duke of York*—it was found necessary to alter the 5·25″ turrets that were firing starshell as the third turrets on the port and starboard side ran out of this type of ammunition. The amount of flashless cordite in the 5·25″ turrets was also limited and after a while the turrets had to resort to using full flash cordite. This provided an excellent aiming point for the *Scharnhorst*'s gunners, which was made full use of. It was found that when the 5·25's checked fire, the accuracy of the *Scharnhorst*'s gunfire deteriorated. It was also noted that the full flash cordite on the 5·25's also caused some discomfiture to the 14″ guns' crews. The forward HA/LA directors were used to control the 5·25″ turrets firing SAP while the after directors controlled those firing starshell.

The three 6″ cruisers were all armed with flashless cordite, but the *Norfolk* had only full flash cordite for her 8″ guns. Again this proved to be quite a hazard, the *Scharnhorst* being able to range on the cruiser with deadly effect. The blinding effect of the fully flashed cordite on the *Norfolk* forced her to use blind fire for her guns, while the *Belfast* and *Sheffield* at times used visual fire, occasionally being able to obtain rather indistinct points of aim.

The shells used by the cruisers in Force 1 also differed. The heavier 8″ shells of the *Norfolk* being set to delay as it was thought that they would be able to penetrate the armour of the *Scharnhorst*. The light 6″ shells of the *Belfast* and *Sheffield* were given impact fuses as it was realised that they would be unable to penetrate the armour of the battlecruiser, and it was thought that in all probability they would be used against German destroyers. On this type of target the 6″ shells could have a deadly effect.

NOTES TO GERMAN GUNNERY AND RADAR

The gunnery radar set mounted aft in the *Scharnhorst* was poor compared to the British sets, and was not nearly accurate enough for the *Scharnhorst* to use "blind fire". Great difficulty was experienced when trying to detect the *Duke of York* as the definition of the set was poor, the closeness of the *Jamaica* to the flagship giving one large blurred echo on the set. In addition to this the set had only a very narrow field of vision, it being necessary to move the whole gear to obtain a picture of the horizon. The echoes received showed up as vertical lines on the radar scope, and from these the range was read off.

The poor definition, however, meant that the accuracy of any bearings thus obtained was never better than 2.

In spite of the defects of her radar, however, the shooting of the *Scharnhorst* was, on the whole, good. Having once got over the initial surprise of being attacked, the *Scharnhorst* employed ripple firing from her main turrets, firing from fore to aft and using impact fused shells. Her ranging was accurate and salvoes were fired at regular intervals.

TABLE 7

21″ TORPEDO ATTACKS

Ship	Time	No. of torpedoes fired	Range	Remarks
Jamaica	19.25	2	3500 yards	C tube misfired due to an improperly closed breech
	19.37	3	3750 yards	Two hits
Belfast	19.27	3	6200 yards	
Matchless		0		Unable to fire tubes
Musketeer	19.33	4	1000 yards	Three hits
Opportune	19.31	4	2000 yards	
,,	19.33	4	2500 yards	
Saumarez	18.56	4	1800 yards	
Savage	18.55	8	3500 yards	Three hits
Scorpion	18.50	8	2100 yards	One hit
Stord	18.50	8	1800 yards	
Virago	19.34	7	2800 yards	Two hits
TOTAL		55		Eleven hits

TABLE 8

RADAR

Ship	Set	Type	No. and Position	Frequency Mc/s	Range (miles)	Remarks
Duke of York	273QR	S/W	1. On top of control tower	3000	20+	Detected *Scharnhorst* at 45500 yards. Standby S/W set.
	281	A/W-S/W				Detected aircraft at 35 miles and surface target at 12¾ miles. Rotating aerial put out of action at 17.30.
	284M3	14″ gunnery control	2. One on top of 14″ director fwd and 1 aft.	600		Detected *Scharnhorst* at 30400 yards. Temporary defect 18.24 caused by gunblast.

78

Ship	Set	Type	No. and Position	Frequency Mc/s	Range (miles)	Remarks
	285M3	5·25" gunnery control.	4. Two on directors fwd, two on directors aft.	600		Only reads ranges. Not capable of giving bearings.
	243	Identification of plane TX		179		Works in conjunction with 281.
	253 91 FVI	IFF				
Belfast	273	To detect enemy TX S/W		3000	20+	Detected *Scharnhorst* at 35000 yards. Affected by gunblast at one stage, but promptly dealt with.
	284	6" gunnery control.		600		Suffered serious interference from own R/T.
	285	4" gunnery control.		600		
Norfolk	273	S/W		3000	20+	Put out of action by 11" shell.
	284	8" gunnery control.	1. On 8" director.	600		Damaged by 11" shell.
Sheffield	273QR 284M3	S/W 6" gunnery control.		3000 600	20+	Bearing readings inaccurate due to defective beam switches.
	285M4	4" gunnery control.		600		
Jamaica	272PR	S/W	1. in front of bridge.	3000	20+	Detected *Scharnhorst* at 27500 yards. Put out of action 19.15 for 17 minutes due to gunblast.
	281	A/W	2. On fore & mainmast.	82	100–200	Detected *Scharnhorst* at 25000 yards.
	284	6" gunnery control.		600		Detected *Scharnhorst* at 24000 yards.
	285	4" gunnery control.	3. Fwd (port & stbd on directors) & aft on director.	600		

Ship	Set	Type	No. and Position	Frequency Mc/s	Range (miles)	Remarks
Matchless	271	S/W	1. On foremast.	3000	20+	
	291			214	Plane=20 @ 10000'. Surface 5½	
Musketeer	271	S/W	1. Aft.	3000	20+	
	291			214		
Opportune	291			214		
	285	4" gunnery control.	1. On top of director.	600		U/S
Savage	271	S/W	1. Aft.	3000	20+	
	291		1.	214		
	285	4·5" gunnery control	1. On top of director.	600		
Saumarez	291			214		
	282	40mm gunnery control.	1. On Bofors mounting.	600		
	272	S/W		3000	20+	
	285	4·7" gunnery control.	1. On top of director.	600		
Scorpion	291			214		
	282	40mm gunnery control.	1. On Bofors mounting.	600		
	285	4·7" gunnery control.	1. On top of director.	600		
Stord	272	S/W		3000	20+	
	291			214		Detected *Scharnhorst* at 17000 yards
	285	4·7" gunnery control.	1. On top of director.	600		Detected *Scharnhorst* at 16000 yards
	285					
	282	40mm gunnery control.	1. On Bofors mounting.	600		
Virago	276	S/W				U/S
	285	4·7" gunnery control.	1. On top of director.	600		
	282	40mm gunnery control.	1. On Bofors mounting.	600		

NOTES TO COMMUNICATIONS AND RADAR IN THE BRITISH FORCES

The radio communications between the ships of the British forces worked exceedingly well under poor conditions. A total of five different frequencies were in use, the main one being 210 Kc/s which was used by all vessels over short ranges when involved in the attacks on the *Scharnhorst*, for communicating orders, sighting reports and for urgent messages. For communications over longer distances and principally between Forces 1 and 2 a frequency of 4740 Kc/s was used. Two different frequencies were used for R/T in the convoy and in Forces 1 and 2. Again this was for use over short ranges, the convoy using 2410 Kc/s and Force 2 and later Force 1 using 4000 Kc/s. Force 2 also used a further frequency for reporting shadowing aircraft—viz.: 3000 Kc/s.

The radar, like the radio, proved invaluable in the sinking of the *Scharnhorst*. In one or two cases, however, difficulty was experienced from gun blast, when, just at a crucial moment, contact with the target would be lost as a section of the radar chain broke down due to the shaking-up it was getting.

The main radar set in use was the surface warning Type 273. Varying marks of this set were fitted in most of the warships (see table 8) and gave excellent results. On the *Belfast* accuracy fell off at one stage due to the shaking the set had received from gunblast, but the fault was quickly repaired and the set continued to work efficiently. The *Sheffield* encountered more serious problems with her Type 273QR, but this wasn't until 19.10, by which time she had missed the action due to shaft trouble. The *Norfolk* was unfortunate enough to have her set put out of action by an 11″ shell.

The Type 284 gunnery control set was used on the larger warships for the main armament. This set proved during the action to be rather prone to break-down, and gave varying results. The set on board the *Duke of York* was put out of action for twenty-five minutes by gun blast at 18.35. On board the *Belfast* readings were unobtainable from the Type 284 set from about 12.30 onwards as interference on the 4000 Kc/s frequency from the *Belfast*'s R/T badly affected the tracking of the scope. On the *Sheffield* the Type 284 gave accurate enough ranges but readings of bearings were inaccurate due to defective beam switches, and the set was virtually unserviceable. On the *Norfolk* the 11″ shell again caused serious damage to the radar, destroying a remote bearing tube. Fortunately she had a spare and was able to get her Type 284 working again for the later actions.

In addition to these two types of radar the *Duke of York* and *Jamaica* were also fitted with an A/W set Type 281. As well as acting as a standby S/W set the Type 281 worked in conjunction with a Type 243 which was used to identify aircraft transmissions and show whether they were friendly or hostile. The 11″ shell that passed through the *Duke of York*'s foremast about 17.30 put the rotating aerial of the Type 281 set out of action and with it the Type 243 set.

The surface warning set on the *Jamaica* was a Type 272PR which was also put out of action due to gun blast at 19.23.

On the destroyers the surface warning set in use was the Type 271 and the air warning set the Type 291. The Type 291 gave good results, except on the *Opportune* where it was out of action. The *Opportune* had no Type 271 and thus had to rely on her gunnery radar set Type 285. The *Virago* was the only destroyer fitted with the new Type 276 S/W set, but this too was out of action, the *Virago* also relying on her Type 285 set. On the *Savage* and *Musketeer* the surface warning Type 271 sets were sited aft and masked by the bridge, making it impossible for the destroyers to detect targets that were ahead of the vessels.

TABLE 9
CASUALTIES

Ship	Killed		Wounded	
	Officers	Ratings	Officers	Ratings
Norfolk	1	6	0	5
Saumarez	1	10	0	11
Total	2	16	0	16

Scharnhorst	1803	36 Prisoners of War.

MEDALS

Adm Sir Bruce Fraser awarded the GCB, Order of Suvorov (1st class) (Russian), and created Lord Fraser of North Cape (from the King of Norway).

Rear-Adm Burnett awarded the KBE.

Duke of York	CO awarded DSO.
Jamaica	CO awarded DSO.
Belfast	CO awarded DSO.
Sheffield	CO awarded DSO.
Norfolk	CO awarded DSO and 8 DSM awarded to the crew.
Savage	CO awarded DSO.
Saumarez	Awarded 2 DSO, 2 bar to DSC, 1 Conspicuous Gallantry Medal, 7 DSM and 9 mention in despatches.
Stord	CO awarded bar to DSC.

TABLE 10
LUFTWAFFE UNITS IN NORTHERN NORWAY

In the summer of 1943 five reconnaissance units of the Luftwaffe were based in Northern Norway, based at Trondheim, Tromso, Stavanger and one other base. The units were all equipped with the B &V 138, although in a few cases these were later replaced with the JU 290 or He 177. A standard number of ten to twelve aircraft were maintained by each unit of which there were often only six or seven serviceable. The crew strength often varied quite considerably too, at times the men having only just left the training unit at Copenhagen.

Up until the summer of 1943 losses in the recce units had been comparatively light, but as escort carriers and catapult ships began to sail with the Arctic convoys, losses of the unarmoured B &V 138 rose sharply.

The units were controlled by Fliegerfuhrer North West and were used purely on shipping reconnaissance duties. Flights were often very long, but once having sighted shipping these units were not expected to maintain contact with the convoys, this duty being left to the U-boats of the navy once they had found the convoy and to the attack and shadowing aircraft of the Luftwaffe, if there were any to spare.

Strict radio silence was maintained, only if a convoy or naval ships was sighted was a report made. Any report so made was first sent to the aircraft's home base before being passed on to the other authorities concerned. This often took some time as radio communications in North Norway were poor. No direct contact between Luftwaffe and Kriegsmarine units was available.

The observers on the aircraft were all very able navigators, relying on dead reckoning for fixing positions. Many of these men had been given naval training to assist them with their duties.

Some B & V 138 were being equipped with the Fug 200 Hohentweil Gerat search equipment during the summer of 1943. This was used for detecting shipping, but only a few aircraft were fitted with it. With a power developed of 30 Kw this set was capable of detecting shipping at ranges of 43 miles. It was possible, however, for ships to be detected outside this range if they were using their own radar equipment. The Fug 200 would pick up the transmissions in spite of the fact that it was working on a different frequency. With practice skilled operators could obtain D/F bearings from the wandering blips appearing on the radar screen in the aircraft. In this event the range of detection could be as great as 105 miles.

TABLE II

WEATHER CONDITIONS
Beaufort wind scale

No.	Velocity (knots)	Description
0	0	Calm
1	1 to 3	Light air
2	4 to 6	Light breeze
3	7 to 10	Gentle breeze
4	11 to 15	Moderate breeze
5	16 to 20	Fresh breeze
6	21 to 26	Strong breeze
7	27 to 33	Moderate gale
8	34 to 40	Fresh gale
9	41 to 47	Strong gale
10	48 to 55	Whole gale
11	56 to 65	Storm
12	above 65	Hurricane

Visibility scale

No.	Description	Distance of visibility
0	Dense fog	Up to 50 yards
1	Thick fog	Up to 300 yards
2	Fog	Up to 600 yards
3	Moderate fog	Up to $\frac{1}{2}$ mile
4	Mist or thin fog	Up to 1 mile
5	Poor visibility	Up to 2 miles
6	Moderate visibility	Up to 5 miles
7	Good visibility	Up to 10 miles
8	Very good visibility	Up to 30 miles
9	Exceptional visibility	Visibility over 30 miles

Hours of daylight (nautical light with sun 12° below the horizon)

Latitude	From	To
71	08.17	15.45
72	08.27	15.34
73	08.39	15.23

BIBLIOGRAPHY

History

Eclipse of the German Navy	Thaddeus v. Tuleja
History of the Second World War	Purnell
Schlachtschiff Scharnhorst	H. Bredemeier
Supplement to the *London Gazette* 5/8/47	Adm Fraser's Despatch
The Battle of North Cape	Lt-Cdr M. Ogden
The Kola Run	Vice-Adm Sir I. Campbell KBE, CB, DSO
	Capt D. Macintyre DSO, DSC
The Royal Navy	Keeble-Chatterton
The Russian Convoys	B. B. Schofield
The Second World War	Sir Winston Churchill
The War at Sea	S. W. Roskill
Tragodie Am Nordkap	F. O. Busch

Technical

Brassey's Naval Annual	
British Battleships	Dr O. Parkes OBE, AINA
British Destroyers	E. March
Die Deutschen Kriegschiffe	E. Groner
German Surface Vessels	H. T. Lenton
German Warships of World War II	J. C. Taylor
Janes Fighting Ships	
Warship International	
Warships of World War II	H. T. Lenton and J. Colledge
Weyers Taschenbuch der Kriegsflotten	